Travels
in an
American
Imagination

2005
Colleen,
We live in a wondrous time.
Lee Foster

Travels
in an
American Imagination

The Spiritual Geography of Our Time

LEE FOSTER

Foster Travel Publishing
Berkeley, California

Editing by Jim Gebbie
Cover Design by Samantha Glorioso

Publisher's Cataloging-in-Publication
(Provided by Quality Books, Inc.)
Foster, Lee, 1943–
Travels in an American imagination : the spiritual
geography of our time / by Lee Foster.
    p. cm.
    LCCN 2004099007
    ISBN 0-9760843-0-9

    1. Foster, Lee, 1943—--Travel.   2. Voyages and travels. 3. Spiritual life.   I. Title.
    G530.F63 2005   910.4
                               QBI05-200013

Foster Travel Publishing
P.O. Box 5715
Berkeley, CA 94705
(510) 549-2202
www.fostertravel.com

Printed in China

This book is dedicated to my three children,
Bart, Karin, and Paul,
major joys in my life, the life force surging forward.

Table of Contents

❦

Introduction

❧

I often feel that I am fortunate to live in one of the most remarkable times ever to be alive. About 300 generations of my human species have flourished since the dawn of civilized life. I believe that my era, in the second half of the 20th century and moving now into the 21st, is a special time.

My era is wondrous. So many advances have occurred technologically in such a short time that the story is stunning. Only now can humans fly easily around the world, communicate instantly over huge distances, and even view our planet from the perspective of outer space, showing its lovely, lonely, blue-green appearance. Only at this time can humans replace hearts or other body parts in an effort to extend life.

But my era is also among the most horrific. The pain and risk that the average human being experiences worldwide is high. The problems that confront man in my time are huge. My species has not controlled its numbers sufficiently through voluntary means. Humans quarrel over finite resources. The world environment is in general decline during my era, with many species going extinct, even as a more thorough knowledge of the environment is evolving.

The hatred of human beings for people of other religions and ethnic groups is high. Technology of mass destruction is becoming widespread. I awake each morning, especially in the 21st century, somewhat fearful about learning the news of the day, which might just be very bad news.

I am preoccupied with both aspects of the question about life today, "What is wondrous and what is horrific about life in our time?" I suspect that many of my compatriots are asking the same question.

If I better understand both aspects of life today, perhaps I (and my readers) can achieve some inner peace when surveying the current human drama.

If I look squarely at life, with unflinching clarity, yet with sufficient imagination, striking a balanced perspective, perhaps only then can I continue living in a healthy, constructive manner and not be overwhelmed by pessimism and despair.

I am expert only on the experience of my own life, but I hope that my observations will resonate with the lives of the Everyman and Everywoman of my era. I feel that every person must find in the details of his or her own life an assessment of what is wondrous and what is horrific about modern life. This book presents an examination of my life as a starting point to assist in and possibly provoke the discussion.

I am basically an optimist. I enjoy the beauty of nature and the story of human history. I believe that the human animal is an astonishing creature. However, I am also a realist who understands that the tragic and disturbing trends of my era may continue. The human animal has both the noblest opportunities for greatness and the greatest chances for catastrophic failure of all the creatures that have evolved on Earth.

I believe that I am in a special position to make this assessment of my time. Born in Minnesota, I began life with a strong sense of place and with a few good people around me, who loved me. I received the finest education possible at Notre Dame and Stanford. As an adult, living in Oakland/Berkeley, California, I have had an opportunity to lead a normal life, raising a family and paying off my mortgage. My chosen field of endeavor, that of a journalist, especially as a travel writer/photographer, has allowed me to travel widely, affording a comparative perspective.

Moreover, no one else has defined my era to my satisfaction. I have caught glimpses of insight in many other descriptions, but no others satisfy me with their portraits. So it will be up to me to make a definition. My own life and thoughts are interesting not for anything eccentric or accidental, but only in so far as they parallel the thoughts and lives of other human beings of my time.

I have written many books/articles and created numerous photographs about the geographic places on the planet. This will be my perspective on the spiritual geography of our era.

My audience, I hope, will be the people of today and the people living 500 years hence, whoever seeks an understanding of these times. This book, written as I pass 60, will serve as a sequel to my earlier book about growing up in a Minnesota America at mid century, titled *Just 25 Cents and Three Wheaties Boxtops,* written in my 20s.

The Osborne computer, circa 1980

CHAPTER ONE

Oakland:
The Rapid Pace of Change

~

The year was 1980, and I had just purchased a new device, packaged in a gray suitcase and developed by an entrepreneur named Adam Osborne, who lived up the street. Little did I comprehend that the device would change my life. The new contraption was a computer, and this model had everything required for me to write and then revise my writing and print out a fresh manuscript. Moreover, it was portable or at least "luggable" and could be hooked up to the phone to make a transmission of the writing to an editor or an audience.

By 1983 I became a part of the new computer publishing revolution by signing a contract with CompuServe to put all my travel writing online in return for a 10 percent royalty. I was the first travel writer ever to publish profitably in the new electronic online computer age. My relationship with CompuServe continued for the next 18 years.

In 1978 I first saw a consumer computer, an Apple II, at the cottage of my beloved father, Russell Foster, on Lake Washington in Minnesota. My father, who was always so fascinated with new technology, said to me, "Type in an article of yours, print it out, take it out on the porch with a glass of wine, revise the manuscript, then come back to the computer and make the changes in the file. Then you can print out the new version."

I had traveled cross-country with my family in our VW camper and was working on an article about the wonders of Yellowstone. I did as my father instructed, found the results magical, and marveled at the new printout. I saw immediately how this new tool could greatly increase my productivity.

Much of my career as a journalist was destined to be involved in publishing using the new technology, first in the online scene and then on the Internet. A company called Ebook published *California,* a CDROM of my work, in 1992, combining a book-length travel text and more than 700 photos on a single disk, a revolution at the time.

By 1995 my website for Foster Travel Publishing (www. fostertravel.com) presented my travel writing/photography for 200 worldwide destinations. The website won Lowell Thomas Awards, including my being named Lowell Thomas Travel Journalist of the Year (Silver Winner).

There were many revolutions occurring simultaneously in Oakland/Berkeley 1975–1985. The real-world issues of the day seemed more compelling to me then than the fiction that I had pursued a few years earlier. My novel, *The Message of April Fools,* about being young, at Stanford, and on the home front in the Vietnam War, was followed in my literary output by nonfiction books, articles, and photographs.

One revolution involved food production. I and others were alarmed by a commercial agriculture that created food with little regard for the effects of pesticides and herbicides on people or the environment. DDT buildup had reached a concentrated high point at the top of the food chain. One unexpected result was that the eggshells of birds became brittle as the birds accumulated DDT in their bodies, preventing successful hatching. The peregrine falcon, a raptor, was in danger of going extinct in the western United States. I became a proponent of organic gardening and raised most of the vegetables for my family of five on a small hillside city lot in the salubrious microclimate of the Rockridge area of Oakland. My book *Backyard Farming* and my articles in Rodale's *Organic Gardening* magazine celebrated these trends, which became mainstream by the end of the century.

Another revolution involved energy production and conservation, an issue related to food growing because homegrown food was so energy-efficient to create. Energy was in short supply and expensive in the late 1970s. I had on my roof one of the first solar hot water units. I cooked my food with a parabolic solar cooker rather than using fossil fuel. I made an effort to recycle everything possible, something that was not popular in that time. The ideal was to live well using as little energy as possible. I and others, such as Sim Van der Ryn, the California State Architect, supported a model house in the Berkeley flatlands, known as the Integral Urban House, which reflected all these visions and practices.

Man's ability to innovate, stimulated partly by need and partly by imagination, continues to amaze me. I often think back on human history and those changes that have so affected mankind, such as the invention of light to banish the dark. First by oil lamps, then gas lamps, and now electric bulbs, the daylight hours can be effectively extended. My era is particularly full of invention and its dramatic effect. I wonder if I and my fellow human beings can manage the changes wisely, especially those involving genetic manipulation. Each new invention has its own set of tensions. Television, for example, places every disaster around the world directly in my face, impossible to ignore, whether the event was the Vietnam War, the first televised war, or the perpetual starvation status of millions of people in sub-Saharan Africa.

Dawn in Jerusalem

CHAPTER TWO

Jerusalem: The Loss of Faith

I stood at the Wailing Wall in Jerusalem observing the Jews in communion with their God. Notes stuck in the wall as prayers were believed to go more instantly to God. Some of the faithful had prophylactic straps around their arms, the tightened constraints testifying to their fervor.

An hour later I walked through the Blue Mosque that is one of the holiest places for Muslims, only a few hundred yards from the Wailing Wall. I left as one of the prayer times of the day approached and the Muslim faithful prostrated themselves on prayer rugs, facing Mecca.

Still another hour later I was strolling the Way of the Cross that Jesus of Nazareth had supposedly walked on the path to his crucifixion.

My own religious journey began in an enriched Catholic environment in Minnesota. I was an altar boy who learned the rituals, singing Latin hymns in the choir. I was surrounded by Jesuit priests and by nuns who taught me. The liturgy was rich in music, incense, and visual stimulation. I narrated on radio the midnight Mass at Christmas. Living in this intensely religious community of Catholics, I came close to becoming a priest, but decided instead to go on to Notre Dame and read the Great Books and then to Stanford as a graduate student in Literature.

Somewhere along the line I totally lost my faith. It happened in college. I no longer believed. I was unable to make the leap successfully from Heaven and Hell as real to Heaven and Hell as imaginary metaphors. Of course, I was humble enough to know that I might be wrong and all the believers might be right, so I was not apostolic about this loss of belief. It was a quiet, private loss. However, I couldn't fake it. Unless a bolt of lightning knocked me off my horse, I could not bring myself to believe.

The loss of faith had many consequences. I lost that easy sense of camaraderie that the faithful have with each other. I missed the sense of community when I moved to California for my graduate studies because there was no church group I felt comfortable with. I raised my own children without any religious passion, teaching them respect for religions and for the capacity of the human imagination to deal with pain and suffering by creating gods. I did not require them to master the trappings of religious culture, such as the Bible literature, which was so much a part of Western Culture.

As life proceeded, I often wondered what I believed in. I certainly did believe that life was a wondrous matter and its origin an unimaginable phenomenon, but without any personalized god involved. I believed I would live on, in some small way at least, in the gene pool I contributed to and the culture that I nourished, both by my deeds and my acts of writing and photography. I believed that life was fundamentally good and joyous, even though the challenges of my time might make life a vale of tears for many people. I believed that service to mankind and the joy of learning about nature and mankind's many cultures would occupy every moment of my life with full intensity when I rose above the pedestrian tasks of providing for myself and my family.

There were many times when I sorely missed the solace of belief. When faced with an untimely death, acts of evil, or random violence, I wished I could turn over all these complexities to the simplifying concept of a god, but I could not. The tensions in my spirit could have perhaps been relaxed if I were a believer whose god was definitely in charge, possibly also all knowing, maybe all wise, and hopefully even a loving god. No such being emerged for me.

I wished I could have given my children a further sense of purpose and social cohesion in a religious setting, but I could not.

In moments when life felt flat and lacking in dimension, I sometimes wished I could infuse life with the radiance that believers sometimes feel. However, that would have been a fabrication for me.

I lived out this lack of belief in relative isolation. I did not try to gather other nonbelievers around me or form some new secular religion. My spiritual life was defined more by the loss than by any action to create a new pseudo belief.

I knew that belief could be a powerful energy source, which caused cathedrals to be built and which sent missionaries to explore the far corners of the earth, all in the name of baptizing the heathen or of generally spreading a vision of the perceived truth. I realized that I would need a different kind of energy source to animate my life.

Believers sometimes had extraordinary discipline and purpose, all due to the presumed righteousness of their cause. I would need to draw on other resources, which I hoped would be as sustaining.

A dancer in Bali

CHAPTER THREE

Bali: The Search for Community

∾

As I watched the Monkey Dance in Bali, all the village dancers seemed to move in unison. They were like a school of fish that magically senses the place of the others and can change direction as a whole, even abruptly. By day the dancers were probably toiling with each other in the rice terraces, cooperating in the planting and watering of their crops, as their ancestors had farmed for centuries. They practiced the same Hindu religion. Now they were dancing together, as if one unit, rather than many individuals.

Their dance was as powerful a sense of community as I had experienced. I often wondered, as life progressed, what caused cohesiveness in the modern world.

In my Berkeley scene the setting was congenial, but the sense of community did not always have continuity. There was little "glue" holding things together.

I did not belong to a church that would provide a sense of togetherness.

For awhile I was one of a group of parents who formed a community around raising their children, but eventually the children went off to college and the participants disbanded.

In earlier decades I would sometimes join groups that enjoyed pleasurable activities, such as drinking wine, but the whims of pleasure were a tenuous bond.

I and others united around causes, such as organic gardening, but when the cause matured, the righteous togetherness diminished.

The people I grew up with remained in Minnesota, and the ties eventually disintegrated. The people I went to school with at Notre Dame and Stanford moved in directions other than my own. Many of them stayed sequestered in academia, while I decided to survive in the rough-and-tumble marketplace world of creating and selling literary or photographic artifacts. I was a freelancer who worked at home. I did not go to an office every day and was not part of a corporation.

What I found, as life proceeded, was that my truest community was composed of those people who did what I did: my fellow travel writers and photographers. My main group was the Society of American Travel Writers. At one point I was Chairman of the Freelance Council, the largest branch in the Society. I also enjoyed a local group of travel writers, the Bay Area Travel Writers. My third community was the American Society of Media Photographers. I kept in touch with these writers and photographers at meetings, on the road as we did trips together, and through emails.

Beyond these groups, I did not have significant other ties. Consequently, I cherished the tribal clusters of which I was a part.

Of course, there were some comforts in the lack of a tight community. The main benefit was the anonymity and privacy possible. No one was watching over me. No one was inhibiting me from any thought or behavior. There was a special sense of freedom in the lack of community.

The underlying cohesiveness that did exist in Northern California showed itself when disaster struck. I had seen this in the 1989 Loma Prieta earthquake. Huge resources could be assembled quickly to assist the victims. Strangers assisted strangers, connected via the media. There was nothing like a disaster to cause neighbors to become acquainted. In fact, there was a strong safety net of invisible protectors around me. If I had a health problem like a heart attack or security problem like a house break-in, the Berkeley fire department and police would arrive in a couple of minutes.

At times, there were somewhat satisfying sport fan communities in which I participated. I could lose myself briefly in front of the TV set when the San Francisco 49ers played football each autumn. My son Paul and I would barbecue some steaks on the grill and debate whether a new quarterback like Jeff Garcia could ever equal the legendary Joe Montana. I could get a little wild and crazy during the tenser moments of certain games, but I was not a logo-wearing fan. When the game ended, the illusion of togetherness passed from me.

Each evening, while preparing dinner, I would watch the evening news, Peter Jennings and then Dan Rather, or else Jim Lehrer on the PBS station, depending on what was being covered. When I watched the evening news, I enjoyed being part of the larger national village of viewers.

When major elections were held in the United States every four years, I had a satisfying sense of being a member of the body politic. When terrorists attacked America on 9-11-01, I was one of the many who felt violated.

There was no doubt that I was a part of several loosely defined communities. But one issue was the intimacy of my relationships with others in my scene. At times I envied the Monkey Dancers of Bali. What I perceived in them was a closeness to others stronger than a modern man in Berkeley, California, was likely to experience.

A summer day in Minneapolis

CHAPTER FOUR

Minneapolis: The Sense of Place

~

M ankato, south of Minneapolis, was the place that meant everything to me early in life. On Sunday afternoons I hiked the green hills and the river bottom woodlands with my father. We shot our rifles and cooked hamburgers in tinfoil over an open fire. In the autumn, as the chill of winter approached, we gathered up our shotguns and walked the crackling, dry rows of cornfields, hoping to flush out a pheasant. With my high school buddy, Tom, I canoed the Blue Earth River or spent a day at Lake Washington fishing for crappies and black bass.

This was the landscape and these were the people that were my sense of place. The fundamental decision of my life was that I left this place and these people, never to return. I moved to California, to Stanford and then to Oakland/Berkeley.

For a couple of decades I drifted back occasionally. My parents were alive then. There were some high school reunions, but eventually that tradition died.

There were some things that I missed about Minnesota and other aspects I could easily live without. I didn't miss the severe, snow-shoveling winters, the hot and muggy summers, and the mosquitoes of Minnesota. I would not voluntarily go back to that. My father had delighted in this "theatre of the four seasons," but I preferred the mild, dry, sunny, and cool climate of Berkeley.

I missed the people of Minnesota, their voices, their sensibilities. When I heard that voice on the telephone, that German-Irish-Scandinavian-Lutheran-Catholic voice, that slight r on the end of long words, I felt a pang of nostalgia and also a special comfort level.

My neighbors in Berkeley, by chance, were an extended Ethiopian family who had migrated to the United States and had done well. Their children mixed with my children at the Berkeley High School and at the University of California. They were good people, cultured and well educated, but they were also so different from me that a natural barrier kept the contact somewhat distant. Among Minnesotans I never felt such a barrier.

I liked the opportunities that California presented. In my California, it seemed, everyone had written a book or had done something interesting in technology, business, or the arts. Everyone seemed in pursuit of something intriguing. My first apartment-mate at Stanford, for example, was a student of the history of music, focused on recreating the harpsichord music of the 17th century. In California one was free to do or be whatever one had the talent and vision to pursue.

Probably the watchful community awareness of Minnesota would have suffocated me. My Minnesota seemed to be either corn or soybeans, and what would I do with them? I could have worked with my father in his factory, but I would have wished to escape the work for what I perceived as loftier creative pursuits.

There were many forces destroying the sense of place in my time. My era saw the triumph of the franchise concept, with McDonald's as the most successful example.

When inside a McDonald's, one could be anywhere. Both the décor and the food were totally replicable.

The variations of the human voice in different American places also tended to diminish in my time and a new homogenization of speech occurred, as more people spent more of their time listening to the standardized voices of the national media persons on TV and radio.

It also became more difficult, with each passing year, to approximate what was in the mind of a person from a given place. That person may have logged hours a day absorbing the thoughts and attitudes of TV or Internet content from an entirely different place.

The Berkeley world my children grew up in was a place unlike my own Minnesota childhood. In Berkeley the scene was totally multicultural, with all the races and religions mixed together. My son Paul was one of the few white boys on the mostly black basketball team at Berkeley High. Paul didn't seem to notice. There was no dominant religion, not even Christianity, in the Berkeley world of my children, so the Buddhist and the Jew and the freethinker had an equal status in the curriculum and in daily life. All-American festivals like Columbus Day were not celebrated enthusiastically in Berkeley because the arrival of Columbus was a disaster for the Native American. The festival became Native American Peoples Day. My children grew up in a fairly hopeful scene, with everyone understanding what it meant to be a minority or an outsider at one time or another.

Once I was having dinner in a San Francisco restaurant with my offspring, who were in grade school. Into the restaurant came a group of young people from a private school choir in Minnesota. As I thought of my own children, with the joys and challenges of their multicultural world of Berkeley, with all its rich diversity, I also recognized the easy familiarity of these homogenized, monocultured young people from Minnesota, at ease with themselves.

Plaza in colonial Alamos, Mexico

CHAPTER FIVE

Mexico: The Tentativeness of Love

~

I had driven my VW Bug across the Sonora Desert of Mexico, doing some annual travel editorial research. I was headed for the preserved colonial city of Alamos in the state of Sonora and the restaurant of my friend, Senor Luis, whom I enjoyed visiting each year to catch up on matters Mexican.

When I arrived at his restaurant, she was there. She was possibly the loveliest young woman I had ever seen in Mexico. She was the best and brightest young person then in bloom in the village of Alamos and had been befriended by Luis's family. She was working in his restaurant as a way to get out of Alamos to the great world beyond. I was free at the time, in my 20s, and we fell for each other passionately.

But I was cautious also. I would not risk an accidental pregnancy. I wondered how this beautiful girl from Mexico would fare in the foreign world of California. The meeting ended indecisively, with mutual longing and desires unfulfilled.

My life, from 18 to the present, has always been a search for love with a woman. I would never have survived as a celibate in the Catholic priesthood.

My most satisfying long-term love has been for Anke, a Dutch woman, the mother of my children. Tragically, that relationship did not survive, due to the aftermath of a medical disability that Anke suffered, a matter discussed in the chapter "Amsterdam: The Intrusion of Tragedy."

My other relationships with women never lasted. In my 20s I had a desire to create a life in the arts, doing writing and photography for sale, a risky matter, so the tension of remaining free to create always conflicted with the stability needed for long-term romance and family formation.

In my 30s and 40s, I experienced relative calm in my life with Anke. After Anke, the turmoil returned, and I eventually accepted that this was the norm of man-woman relationships in my time. Several things seemed to affect the picture.

Secure birth control, which was new in my time, enabled my partners to go through adult life without much risk of unplanned pregnancy. I had managed to get through Catholic high school in Minnesota without an accident as this technology became known. In my 50s a vasectomy resolved the issue for me for all time.

The fear of AIDS and other sexually transmitted diseases made sex a basically defensive act after about 1990. One never knew if a partner's fleeting encounter earlier might have messed them up with something like herpes, or worse.

When men and women were not interested in having children, and many were not in my time, the need to form a family unit with a long-term romance relationship was meager.

Adults of both sexes in my time were more wedded to their career paths than to each other. Careers took unexpected directions, people grew and changed, friendships came and went, so it was little wonder, in all this flux, that romance was also impermanent.

Women in my time had near parity with men in most professions, making them fiscally independent. Surviving financially as a single person was an option that women had not enjoyed in earlier eras. Women worked hard to develop their independent professional status. A relationship needed to have extraordinary romantic appeal for it to continue, given that there was no financial necessity for being together.

In my 50s I briefly married Mary Lou, a beautiful woman from Tampa, Florida, who joined me in California in the travel writing/photography world. We both thought that it would be easy for her to conclude that the Bay Area of California was a more congenial place to live than Florida. But we were wrong. The tug of family, friends, and the place she had grown up, and knew and loved, won out. This helped convince me that a long-distance romance with a woman deeply rooted in another place was not likely to succeed.

Perhaps my next romance would be with someone I would meet on an Internet intro service, such as Match. com. I would specify my ZIP code 94709 and seek a woman only within a radius of 20 miles. On a certain night, I went into Match.com and put in these variables. There were about 50 women ages 40–60 listed on that day, on that service, within the specified mile radius, who identified themselves as looking for a man like me, then age 59. I had to concede that all this searching had its comic aspects.

I hoped that romance would last forever, and I was prepared to be pleasantly surprised if it happened. I am basically an optimist, who believes she might appear one day. I will be on the lookout for her.

South Window in Arches National Park

CHAPTER SIX

Utah: The Joy of Family

The temperature hit 105 degrees in Arches National Park as Anke and I, with our three children—Bart, Karin, and Paul—pulled into the campground. I got out for a hike, leaving the tribe in the air-conditioned comfort of the 26-foot-long Mini Winnie RV. They could retrieve a chilled beverage from the fridge or warm up a hot dog in the microwave while watching dad do his photos in the searing afternoon heat. By evening the heat dissipated, and the cheerful tribe emerged from the RV cocoon. We watched the stars that night against a darkened sky with no light pollution. It was one of many memorable trips I did with my children.

Having children was one of the better decisions of my life. I was late in starting a family, partly because I needed to stay unencumbered to launch a literary career and partly because I was influenced at Stanford by Paul Ehrlich, the population biologist, who made everyone feel guilty about procreating.

Family members are the most solid people in my life. My four sisters and my three children are there for me. They will always be there, through thick and thin. I will always be connected to them.

My parents died too young, in their 70s, of cancer and other maladies, in Mankato, Minnesota, where the health care providers, I feel, were not always the most competent. Then my sisters and I became the final generation. This was a sobering and maturing experience. This was it, there was no longer a time of preparation, this was the final act, though it would be prolonged for decades.

Every year for about 15 years, after my mother died, my four sisters and I gathered together for a Family Reunion. We came from as far away as Indonesia and Minnesota to a designated place in California, Oregon, Hawaii, or Minnesota. Our spouses or significant others came too, as did our children. Spouse Tom, husband of my sister

Sheila, made a video recording of the family-reunion collective history and presented a copy to everyone. Eventually, as the years passed, far-flung children could not always attend. Health issues and busy schedules affected the Reunion, which became reduced to a "gathering" of smaller groups, perhaps only a few of the family at one time, when the "core" group of five siblings could not make it.

I was the patriarch who organized the Reunions. It was a time for all the members to bond, within and across the generations. We rafted and hiked together, we saw Shakespearean plays, we relaxed at great resorts, and always we sought out a lodging where we could cook feasts. We liked to prepare food together. Friends and professional associates came and went in my life, but my family remains forever.

Having children in my era is unlike any earlier time. For one thing, children take a great deal of support to be launched properly. To me, they need to be well educated, with a bachelor's degree at least. Youngsters also have many opportunities that exceed even the enlightened world where I grew up in Minnesota. My children were able to spend part of almost every summer in the Netherlands, for example, affording a comparative cultural experience. In high school, my daughter Karin served in the Amigos de las Americas organization, taking health care education to villages in South America, spending one summer in Paraguay and another in Brazil.

Sons and daughters also help parents in my era to connect with and function in the modern world. When the dsl on my computer crashes, I am fortunate to have my son Paul to solve it. My son Bart was already making electronic Christmas cards for family members on his Apple Computer, with photos and music, in the mid 1980s. Young people have a facility and delight with the new technology that often exceeds the skills of their parents.

I watched as my children displayed the survival skills that were necessary for their lives. My daughter Karin weathered a seizure disorder, not allowing it to slow her down in getting her graduate degree at Johns Hopkins in Government Policy, with an Environmental emphasis. My son Bart carved out an entrepreneurial career consulting in the telecommunications industry, able to function as a manager of projects for AT&T and Airtouch. They needed Bart's skills at a high fee even as they were downsizing their own staff. My son Paul graduated in Information

Technology from the University of California Santa Cruz just as the dot-com bubble burst. Paul had to scrounge for employment until he landed a good job at the investment firm of Franklin Templeton. These young adults knew that they would have to prove their worth, daily, in a competitive environment.

As I grow older, the irrepressible exuberance of youth, the life force that youth represents, is a helpful counterbalance to the caution that weighs upon me. Despite all the problems in the world, my children have gone on to have their own offspring and proceed with their lives. I had more of that energy when I was younger. As I pass 60 I would not have the courage to create new life again. I will leave that up to the next generation.

Downtown Orlando

CHAPTER SEVEN

Orlando: The Importance of Friends

∾

We meet only once a year, late each spring, this group of five friends, but it is an important connection for me. We are professional colleagues, some of the main travel writers of our time. We also like each other's company. We have seen the world together and separately. Moreover, we all share a mission—to improve the travel writing scene for the next generation of young writers and photographers coming up. So we formed an entity, the Institute for Travel Writing and Photography, to impart the best practices to about 25 aspirants each spring. I hosted the group one year in San Francisco. One member, Herb, who lives near Orlando, ended up hosting the group for five years in Florida.

I keep up my participation in the group meeting each spring in Orlando, partly for the pleasure of seeing my fellow faculty members. They are the people doing what I do. They are among my best friends. Tom, from Boston, is the world authority on Turkey, having written for many years the definitive book on that area for Lonely Planet. Herb, from Florida, is known as the ecological conscience of Florida tourism. Tim, also from Florida, is an expert writer and photographer on the Caribbean. And Bruce, from California, has established a respected series of books on Mexico with Avalon Publishing. Every year, after the Institute, we pause for a leisurely dinner together and share our thoughts about life passing.

Friendship in my time takes on some new characteristics. I live in the electronic age, and friendship has become electronified, with many ramifications. One aspect is that the email replaces the letter and the phone call. This means that it is possible to communicate instantly and over remote distances with friends. But the email is also a silent communication, the phone does not ring, though the email could indeed be a voice message if one wished. The email can be dashed off, without the more deliberate dialogue required of the earlier form of communication, the letter. Email is a different kind of animal from a phone conversation, which actually demands that two people, at a precise moment, pay immediate attention to each other.

Friendship, I have learned, can be easy and automatic when one is young, but it becomes a more voluntary act in later years. I have seen my children "make friends" in an instant, bonding with a new child on the block. In my own 20s and 30s, I could be "thrown together" with people who loved literature, for example, and make friends easily. After age 50, friendship has become more a matter of purposeful choice, requiring leisure time and will.

One paradox of my life is that my best friends do not live in the neighborhood. They live far away. I often wish that they were closer, so I could drop in to spend time with them. They are travel writers or travel photographers, roaming the globe, meeting and bonding in faraway places. I remember looking at China with my friend from Colorado, Steve.

Another aspect of friendship in my time is how frequently people move. I saw this affect my three children, especially my son Paul, the youngest. As Paul grew up in the Rockridge area of Oakland/Berkeley, families moved in and out. Paul would make friends, then the family would move. Families moved partly because of the schools. The grade school in our Oakland neighborhood, Chabot School, was excellent, but the Oakland high schools were a problem. So families would move when their children reached junior high school age. I established my address in Berkeley, as my own family went through reorganization, partly so my children could go to the better Berkeley middle and high schools. My children did not have continuity in friends, which perhaps prepared them for a reality of adult life—that people would be moving, rather often.

As I grow older, sometimes earlier friends cycle back, which brings me much pleasure. My friend Elton, for example, was an executive at Sunset Publishing who shared my own literary sensibility. Elton moved to Seattle and joined Microsoft, where he took charge of Bill Gates's book operations for a decade. Elton and I fell out of touch. Then, one day, Elton called and reconnected, lamenting the neglect of our friendship. We both felt that something had been lost, but we would now try to recover it.

In my adult world in Berkeley, there is more "association" than friendship. For example, I am a member of the Berkeley YMCA, where I love to go in the evening at 9 P.M. and do some cardio and weights while listening to music. It is my relaxing exercise time of the day. There are an amazing 11,000 people who became members of this downtown Berkeley Y, a facility with state-of-the-art pools, cardio equipment, and weight rooms. The people are a mix of everything, of all races, ages, religions, languages, and backgrounds. It is a kind of ideal world, of people getting along and taking good physical care of themselves. But it is also more of an association of people, who are quite different from each other and give each other space and respect. I associate with people at the Y, but I would not call the people there my friends.

Amsterdam canal houses

CHAPTER EIGHT

Amsterdam: The Intrusion of Tragedy

∽

*T*he flower parade was overpowering both in its visual effect and its perfume. I was at the Bloemencorso, the every-10-year parade in Amsterdam, celebrating the beauty of flowers in the Netherlands and the huge industry of flower production. But amid all this floriferous celebration something was terribly wrong. My partner, Anke, was unconscious in the hospital. I had been at the hospital for the past day, but the doctor had asked me to take a break, get some fresh air in the city, there was nothing I could do.

I had just flown into Amsterdam from Mazatlán, Mexico, where I had been doing some travel research. Anke met me at the airport. We were in good spirits. But, as we drove into the city, Anke experienced a medical crisis, what was called a "tubal pregnancy." She began bleeding internally. We went to an emergency hospital, at midnight on a Sunday. The hospital's resources were down. It took awhile to diagnose the problem. A timely operation was critical. They didn't have Anke's correct blood type for transfusions. The doctors weren't at the top of their game. During the operation Anke had a heart stoppage and went into a coma. The coma lasted three weeks, but she came out of it. However, her speech and left arm function were impaired. She gradually recovered enough for us to return to the United States and continue our lives. Anke, a gifted linguist, found her speech never recovered, a great tragedy for a woman who spoke four languages and would have taught Dutch at the University of California, Berkeley.

This was the biggest tragedy that had ever occurred to anyone close to me in my life. Anke and I went on to vote for the future. We created two more children together. But the tragedy of the event continued to impinge on our lives. Anke struggled on, but there was understandable anger and frustration over how life was turning out. In the years that followed, tensions arose over this major disappointment in life. The stress proved more than the two of us could endure together.

I saw a lot of tragedy in the lives of others as I traveled and lived in my time. Deeply rooted in my American temperament was a wish to deny tragedy's unfolding impact on life. An American seems to be always looking for the newly sprouting wildflowers in the spring after the devastating forest fire of the year before. However, I gradually learned that, with humans, the tragedy sometimes tends to become compounded, rather than resolved, and it cycles back to haunt one years later.

There were both slow-moving tragedies and swift tragedies in the world I saw around me.

I drove every day through Berkeley from my small condo in North Berkeley to my post office mailbox in the Rockridge area. When I drove through the flatlands of Berkeley, I saw the under-served, those whose education, health care, and other basic needs had never been met. I thought often of the irony that in this job-rich (at least at times) Silicon Valley–enhanced region the high tech

companies pleaded effectively with the Immigration reg-
ulators to let in more skilled foreign workers from Asia.
Employers argued there weren't enough locals with the
educational level to fill the jobs. I saw the homeless locals
pushing their shopping carts, looking for the stray alumi-
num can to recycle for a profit, and I felt how unfinished
and imperfect was the American egalitarian vision. I had
known the relatively smug comfort of places like Stanford
and Palo Alto, but my heart was always with the more
struggling elements of the society and their daily efforts
to survive.

I also experienced some fast-moving tragedies. I remember the nervousness of people in Yugoslavia when I
passed through about a year before the collapse of their
state. I was in Zagreb and Belgrade and the lovely seaside town of Dubrovnik. Something was terribly wrong.
The inflation rate was running at 2,000 percent. People
got their paychecks at 3 P.M. on a Friday afternoon and
rushed to the bank to change the money into stable German marks. If they waited another hour, the money might
lose another 10 percent. Muslims and Christians eyed each
other in an uneasy truce below the thin veneer of civility.
Various Christian groups began to recall and nurture their

simmering hatred over who had done what to whom in the difficult World War II Hitler era.

One thing new in my time is that the average modern citizen, because of technology, especially TV, becomes aware of tragedy on an unparalleled scale, and one has to factor that into daily life. The devastation wrought on the Indian Ocean countries from the great tsunami of December 2004 played over and over on the TV screens of the worldwide audience. Everyone who doesn't deliberately bury his or her head in the sand knows about a lot of terrible things, but one has to proceed in a constructive way with life, not paralyzed by that reality. Political strife, environmental deterioration, and the personal plight of individual humans worldwide impinge on my sensibility every day. A modern person has to develop certain psychological modes of coping with this, not becoming callous on the one hand, and not becoming mired in useless pity on the other. It is one of the challenges that all modern citizens face, for the first time in the history of our species.

Terra-cotta warriors in Xian, China

CHAPTER NINE

Beijing: The Experience of Being a Minority

～

I was packed into the crowded Beijing subway and all eyes were staring at me. Going from Point A to Point B in this imperial capital, underground, I was the only Caucasian person on the train. The other passengers seemed to view me as an alien exotic. I did not feel fearful because the Chinese culture is not one to encourage theft or physical harm. Rather, I felt a profound loneliness, sensing that I was far, far away from anyone who knew me or cared about me. It was the ultimate minority experience.

I felt like Ishi, the last member of an Indian tribe in California, whose life was recounted in a book. A week later I was walking in Xian, in Central China, amid the 5,000 terra-cotta warriors that a certain Chinese emperor had ordered created to stand guard at his tomb. China was such a vast world unto itself that there was really little of interest to the Chinese, then or now, beyond the border of their country.

There have been times in my life when I felt like the majority and other times when I felt like a minority.

Growing up in Minnesota I was in the majority, though, more correctly, there was no minority. Minnesotans in my town of Mankato grew up with little prejudice because there were no people around different from them. There was no occasion for intolerance. There were few Blacks, Jews, Asians, or Hispanics. This was the tolerant, liberal world of Hubert Humphrey and Walter Mondale. All the people were white, Protestant or Catholic, and probably German, English, Irish, or Scandinavian. It was a world of virtue untested.

In my California world of Berkeley, I am in the minority, in several respects.

I am a white Californian as the population gradually evolves toward a predominately Hispanic state, with strong Black and Asian elements.

I am a white male at a time when women are rising to positions of parity in society.

I am one of the small group of people who actually commit their lives to making a living in the arts, creating and selling writing and photography in my case. I did not situate myself comfortably in academia or in some prosperous business.

As I pass 60, I find myself suddenly a minority in another sense. I am an older person in a world dominated by visions of eternal youthfulness. At some unspecified time my name changed to "Sir." Sometimes the young seem not to notice me. To some I have become irrelevant and they are impatient with me. I qualify for senior citizen discounts, though I take advantage of them with some ambivalence.

Minorities always have to endure some prejudice. I watched with delight on those occasions when talent triumphed over prejudice in my times. I traveled to Georgia and other places in the South, such as Memphis, where

Martin Luther King was killed. In some of these places, a palpable prejudice and institutional racial system lingered.

At the turn of the new century, I watched as Blacks took their rightful place where talent only was the decider. No one could hit the baseball out of the park better than Barry Bonds, or take the ball to the hoop more effectively than Michael Jordan, or slam the tennis ball more adroitly than the Williams sisters, or sink the putt more skillfully than Tiger Woods, who is both Black and Asian (Thai). Tiger has won repeatedly at golf courses that would have banned him, because of race, only a generation ago.

If sport is an access point to equality, it is only the start. The country was being guided, as I wrote this, by Colin Powell and Condolezza Rice. Racial difference, in some higher circles, is finally becoming irrelevant. However, much remains to be done at the lower levels of society in the imperfect world of America. The country is a restless place in my time, committed to ideals, but people are well aware of how imperfectly these ideals have been achieved.

My spirit is entrepreneurial. I believe in the power of the individual to pull oneself up by one's bootstraps. I see

that so much of the creativity in society is based on individual effort, which America has been more successful in
liberating than any other country in my time. But beyond
the more dynamic individuals, who can rise heroically
above adversity, there is also a mass of people who are
restricted by their unfortunate circumstances. I am pain-
fully aware of the conditions that prevent their success.
How can people expect someone to compete well who had
poor nutrition before childbirth, inadequate health care,
a second-rate education, and even a speech environment
that identifies them in an underclass?

I have never been comfortable with the wholesale trans-
fer of huge wealth from one generation to another, there-
by preserving the status quo of privilege over real talent.
I believe that some wealth has to be transferred so as to
unleash the energy of families to provide for their future.
But if I were the political god, I would do more to give each
child in America an equal start in the grand race of life.

A wild jaguar in the Brazilian rain forest

CHAPTER TEN

Brazil: The Decline of the Environment

⌒

While walking in the Atlantic rain forest of Itatiaia National Park, a half day from Rio, I came upon a large bromeliad, a plant whose upward-cupping leaves caught the falling water. The bromeliad lived on the side of a tree, literally in the air. Peering inside, I examined the complex world of this species. Tiny frogs abounded. Insects of many shapes and sizes found niches. Small butterflies flitted about, feeding off the orchids and other flowers living inside. I could see that there were hundreds of species of living things in this one bromeliad.

The plants in this immediate forest were safe, but most of the trees along my drive from Rio had been cut.

The experience was so unlike walking in the great Temperate Zone forests of North America, such as the lodgepole pine stands of Yellowstone. There I saw a few species, replicated over and over. One could cut down that forest or watch it burn, which it had evolved to do every generation or so, and it would regenerate itself intact.

But this tropical rain forest of Itatiaia could never emerge intact if cut or burned. All the species in the bromeliad would be lost forever. Where would the frog wait for a hundred years for the forest to regrow and the host plant to reappear? Where would the butterfly that had evolved over eons to feed on a certain color of orchid wait during the interim regrowth? They would all perish.

One thing I valued in my travels was the tactile sense of the world that was imparted to me, simply by being there. The complexity and fragility of the tropical rain forest was an abstraction until I set foot there. Once there, I could immediately grasp the reality.

The decline of the environment is one of the major experiences of my time. However, the knowledge with which to measure the decline is relatively new. Forces

can be mustered to save species when the will is sufficient. I watched as the California Sea Otter, the Northern
Elephant Seal, and the California Gray Whale gradually returned from the brink to stable numbers. The great
symbol of the American plains, the buffalo, fell from an
estimated 60 million in 1800 to about 1,000 in 1889, but
it is now back to stable and survivable numbers.

I am lucky to live in a relatively healthy environment
every day in Berkeley. I drink some of the purest water
on earth, water right out of the Mokelumne River watershed in the Sierra. I breathe relatively clean air. For food
I can buy the most lovely, varied, and relatively chemically
clean produce available anywhere, both at the standard
Safeway and the upscale Andronico markets in Berkeley/
Oakland.

I often travel to places where people are at great daily
risk due to their local environment. I choked on the exhaust
of cars in Mexico City in January when the inversion layer
trapped the fumes. I saw dust storms in Beijing, caused by
deforestation, virtually shut down the city. In many Third
World situations, I watched women spend large amounts
of their income on a bottle of Coca-Cola for their babies.
They bought this branded drink because it was not

contaminated so as to cause diarrhea, compared to the local water supply. I have seen tribal people on the edge of starvation in the relatively prosperous and fecund world of Kenya, and I could only imagine the human suffering that is occurring elsewhere in Africa.

In Florida I have gone swimming with the manatees. There are only about 2,500 of these large "sea cows" remaining. Ironically, they are identified by the boat scars on their heads and backs because boaters often run over these slow-moving mammals. I saw these huge animals trying to survive in the warm springs to be found amidst housing developments in Florida at Crystal Springs.

Every informed person in my time has to live in some way with the knowledge of environmental deterioration. One has to integrate this awareness into life without simply becoming depressed or incapacitated, which does nothing to affect the situation positively. There is a heavy metaphysical and psychological burden weighing on people of my time who know that 20 percent of the Earth's species have been wiped out forever in just 50 years. Men have become gods, or devils, simply by existing and putting pressure on the world environment.

There are many ways to react, of course. For some, denial is an effective response. Simply ignore these problems, go on with life, and one will eventually die and the problems will continue. I have a special role in my travel journalism to inform people about the world environmental scene, including the opportunities to have small, incremental effects ameliorating the situation. I have watched on cruise ships in Alaska's Glacier Bay as 2,000 people oohed and aahed when an endangered humpback whale spouted off the bow of the ship. These whale watchers are now part of the voting block that assists in protecting the humpback.

In my era, for the first time, people on Earth have seen a picture from space of their fragile planet. I hope Earth's people and environment survive.

Movie star impersonators in Los Angeles

CHAPTER ELEVEN

Los Angeles: The Age of Entertainment

~

Whenever I go to Los Angeles, I am reminded that I live in the age of entertainment. In Los Angeles I might go to an amusement park devoted to entertainment, Universal Studios, which is a movie set. A restaurant at Universal, such as Marvel Mania, has an entertainment theme, this one being the comic strip. The entire city of Los Angeles seems like a movie set. One never knows when one might run into something being filmed for TV or a movie. Everybody in the city seems to have their TVs on at all times, as if the TVs are additional human voices making contact. Beautiful young people skating along the concrete path at Venice Beach have the "look" of potential young stars waiting to be discovered.

I have never been entirely comfortable with the entertainment preoccupation of my time. Personally, I like to do active things, rather than watch. After watching a passive entertainment, I sometimes feel that I have been robbed of my time. There is also the irony that I live in a supposed age of leisure, but I have little leisure. I am an underpaid information and insight worker who has to earn a living. I actually have to work long hours so I don't have much time to be entertained.

Entertainment means so much to the people of my time. It is like a religion. It is what unites them. So many watch the same TV shows that this is an important thing they have in common, possibly the main commonality. A person can meet someone and learn that they both watch the X Files, and there is a sudden bond. The movies people have seen together are another major shared experience. Movies and TV shows are like the classics of literature that all liberally educated persons once knew. They are like the Bible stories known to most educated people of earlier Western Culture or to people in religious enclaves today.

Entertainment is easier to absorb than the effort required to read a book. One simply has to watch.

Sometimes I feel I have fallen so far behind in this watching of entertainment, compared to other people, that I wonder where I should jump in, to catch up, if indeed that is even worthwhile.

Trivial knowledge about the entertainment world is considered valuable. On TV quiz shows people can win a million, it seems, if they know "which popular rock band of the 1960s had a bass player who broke his left leg in a car accident." People care enough about this kind of trivia to absorb it.

The relationships that people have with imaginary characters on TV or in the movies are often more important than their actual relationships with real, live people. I wonder how many people find the characters on the TV shows Friends, Seinfeld, or Frasier more satisfying than the actual people in their lives. Indeed, for many people the range of emotional life that they vicariously experience with these characters is more compelling than the emotional experiences of their own lives. I was in a crowd once when a "celebrity sighting" of Clint Eastwood took away everyone's breath. It was as if a marvelous being from a superior planet had condescended to spend a few moments among mere Earthlings.

In my specialized world of travel writing, entertainment plays a major role. Travelers' eyes light up when they learn that a certain movie has been filmed at a given destination. Suddenly there is something magical about that destination. The movie clearly enhances the reality of the place. Every Convention & Visitors Bureau in the world has at the ready a list of movies made in its area.

America exports entertainment, which is a big part of the story of American cultural dominance around the world. I could be in the Netherlands at the house of relatives and see reruns of the TV series Dallas 10 years later. They were just getting the series then. The world is free to choose its entertainment, and people often choose American products. This is one reason why American English became the universal language of my time, dominating other language groups. This entertainment cultural dominance is also an aspect of the rising resentment against the United States in some quarters.

I watch as Americans gain weight because they request more entertainment and do less active things. The amount of entertainment to choose from is amazing. In my travels

I enjoy staying at hotels that have Cable or Satellite TV because I don't have Cable at my own condo in Berkeley. I find myself flipping through the sometimes 100-plus channels, amazed at the range of material available, perhaps in Spanish as well as English, and maybe in Chinese or other exotic languages. The choice of what entertainment to watch is paralyzing in its complexity. Somehow each of these channels finds its audience, or else it goes off the air. Someone out there is watching all those channels.

It is said by some that only the desire for sex exceeds the desire to be entertained.

Gustav Vigeland's sculptures in Oslo

CHAPTER TWELVE

Oslo:
The Refreshment of Art

❧

I expected to find gamblers, or, more politely, "gam-ers," in Las Vegas, but I did not anticipate an expe-rience of art. Always open to the possible joy of unexpected art, I went to my first Cirque du Soleil show, *Mystere*, in Las Vegas. Would this be just a circus? The performance proved to be something entirely different. It was about the mystery of life, the shock of existence, the joy of sen-suality. Dancers and tumblers and trapeze artists, all with the most dazzling theatrical effects, performed their acts. The show, developed by a Montreal-based company, was scripted in a make-believe Latinate language so that all meaning was conveyed in sound and movement and light rather than recognizable words. From that day on, whenever I could see a Cirque du Soleil performance, I jumped at the opportunity.

I am a believer in art and its ability to enrich the human spirit. In my college years, I had a copy of Picasso's *Guernica* on my walls. I saw the painting in Chicago and felt there was something moving about a modern warlike world out of control in the image. But I also liked Picasso's *Three Musicians*, which was an image about the spirit of art. I also had Renoir's *Luncheon of the Boating Party* on my wall. There was something so satisfying in the painting, about the good life, the sensuality of women, the joy of camaraderie, and the presence of good food and drink.

I recognize that art can ambitiously call into question the perception of life. More often than not, art is bound to fail to be meaningful. I might have to go to 10 concerts before the moment of music that moves me to tears, but that moment will come. I will go to a dozen art openings to discover the one art object that speaks to me.

There were a few times in my life when several of the enriching forces of art came together. I remembered one visit to Washington, D.C., for example, where I saw a couple of hundred George Catlin paintings of American Indians in the 1830s at the Renwick Gallery. This was followed by a night of Shakespeare's *As You Like It* at the Shakespeare Theatre, and on the next day Andrew Lloyd Webber's *Tell Me on a Sunday* at the Kennedy Center. It has been at moments such as this that I have felt a special joy at being alive, and that my life has been enlarged. Art also spurs me on to continue my own creative work.

So much modern art in my time has entirely lost touch with its audience. This is especially true of large artworks in public places, which are often soulless mental exercises. I will endure this because the next art object may be insightful. I am always ready to embrace another meaningful piece of public art. In San Juan, Puerto Rico, I happened upon two notable sculptures, *The Races* and *The Rogativa*. In Oslo I treasured the 200 outdoor nude human sculpture groups by Gustav Vigeland, representing the cycle of life. Vigeland's sculptures are all nude because the artist felt that clothes would have dated them.

Much modern art is a satirical or mindless foisting upon the public of a pointless creation. I can go to a Yoko Ono exhibit at the Museum of Modern Art in San Francisco and wonder why the show is worth mounting, aside from her celebrity status.

Where imagination in urban design or any of the arts flourishes, I am ready to salute it. It might mean saving architecture, such as preserving the Art Deco world of Miami's South Beach. I have also seen totally brutalized and artless urban environments with no imagination whatsoever, such as the Soviet-era concrete apartments of Belgrade. I always enjoy those urban centers that are designing themselves into a congenial environment, such as San Diego's Horton Plaza.

What art is meant to represent is something I know I can only imperfectly grasp because it will always differ from artist to artist. A Huichol Indian I met in Puerto Vallarta, Mexico, held up an elaborately colored mask. Maybe the Huichol was transporting himself, via the mask, to another spiritual realm, possibly recalling moments of hallucinogenic inducement. The White Buffalo dancers at the Native American ceremonials in Gallup, New Mexico, chanted and stepped gravely across the ground. The dance may have been an expression of the life-sustaining buffalo and perhaps a gesture to placate and ease the spirit of the buffalo at the time of harvesting the meat.

My quest for the meaningful art experience might take me to an event nourishing the creation of song, such as the annual Tin Pan South celebration held every April in Nashville. It might mean catching my neighbor from Mankato, Billy, creating his own jazz music with his City Mouse CDs.

The urge to create art is something always of interest to me. I feel it is an audacious act, one better to try at and fail than not to try.

World Trade Center Towers in New York City

CHAPTER THIRTEEN

New York City: The Effects of 9-11-01

❧

*F*rom the top of the World Trade Center Towers, I looked north into Manhattan. The year was 1990, and I was accompanied by a friend in New York City tourism. The view was so impressive, such a concentration in concrete of human energy. So much hard work and ingenuity and prosperity was represented in what lay before me. It was a dramatic view of recent history, of what had been accomplished on this small island in only a little more than 200 years. I gazed down at the American dream expressed for at least a few million people.

A little more than a decade later, the World Trade Center Towers are gone, destroyed by terrorists using an unexpected weapon, commercial airplanes. Like many, I can hardly believe that the event occurred. It was so improbable, so unlikely.

The hostility of large sectors of the world toward America is a new element in my time, only showing itself forcefully around the turn of the 21st century.

There is no inherent or necessary basis for this hostility, I feel, though I can understand aspects of it. America at its best stands for freedom of religion, freedom of political expression, and economic development for all. What is there to argue about that?

I feel that America has become trapped in the accidental aspects of its global power.

America became associated with the Jewish side of the unresolved Jewish-Palestinian issue, when America's enduring interest lay in peace for both parties.

America was seen as anti-Muslim and anti-Arab when America was one of the few countries in the history of countries that sought to guarantee religious freedom and respect ethnic diversity.

America's wealth, accumulated by the hard work and inventiveness of her people, is a source of envy, which is understandable, but the techniques and technology creating that wealth can be replicated elsewhere on the planet.

America's need to deal, as a great power, with the world as it is, means that America has to serve as a source of both inspiration and stability in the world. Sons angry with their own fathers in every country, therefore, see America as a guarantor of the flawed regimes of their fathers.

In the new era of potential mass destruction carried out by terrorists with suitcase-size devices, America can wait to be attacked or try to interdict the problem at its source. America has never before faced such a dilemma.

The key to America's future in the world, I feel, will lie in its ability to convey its virtues, meaning its yearning for democracy and human rights and freedom, without also foisting on the world its lifestyle, which has some elements offensive to other sensibilities. The brazen, in-your-face, overt sexuality of American culture is anathema to much of the Muslim world, as an example. However, they need not emulate that American behavior.

After the turn of the new century, things have become more worrisome for America in the global struggle against terrorism. Even remote enclaves of relative peacefulness are not exempt. In 2002 about 180 innocent people died in a bombing at Kuta Beach in Bali. The bombing shattered the magic and joy I had known in Bali, which is, ironically, a Hindu rather than Muslim enclave. The targets in Bali were mainly Australians. I fear that the news of the day as the years proceed might report far worse examples of terrorism and mass destruction. I worry about the Pakistan-India conflict and the paranoid secretiveness of North Korea. These problems are as volatile as the conflict in the Middle East.

In my adult life there were two defining moments of great danger for the planet. Everybody remembers where they were at those times.

The first was in 1963 when the Cuban Missile Crisis almost provoked a nuclear exchange between the United States and the Soviets. I had already gone through a childhood in the 1950s practicing how to dive under my school desk, as if this might actually assist me in surviving a nuclear attack. During the Cuban Missile Crisis, I was a student at Notre Dame. If that exchange had occurred and a large number of missiles had been fired, civilization as we know it would have been radically altered. In fact, everything good that has happened in the world since 1963 owes its opportunity to the prudence, fear, and restraint that motivated the national leaders of the United States and the Soviet Union, plus the fortunate fact that they could communicate without a glitch in that high testosterone moment in human history.

The second time of danger was 9-11-01, though the event was more a prelude to an era of terrorism than the defining event. On that day I was trapped on the island of Bermuda and couldn't leave it. I remember just wanting to be back home in California.

I am an optimist and will remain one until the final moment when optimism is no longer possible. If that tragic moment occurs, I am prepared to accept an unavoidable fate.

Wildflowers in the Mojave Desert, California

CHAPTER FOURTEEN

Mojave Desert: The Mystery of Time Passing

~

*I*n April, in years when I am fortunate enough to have the opportunity, I go out to Lancaster in the Mojave Desert of California to see the wildflowers. This is one of the great wildflower experiences available on Earth. Poppies begin at my feet and end at the horizon. Lupine, coreopsis, and other flowering plants flourish all around the town of Lancaster and at Saddleback Butte State Park. The flowers renew themselves each spring, as they have done from time immemorial, a life force exerting itself forward, oblivious to my presence or existence.

The mystery of time passing, the reality of the immutable life force surging onward, the joy of my own brief moment of existence, the sheer beauty of plant life all around me during spring in the desert—all these thoughts absorb me at Lancaster in the spring during the flowering time.

Sometimes, after Lancaster, I enjoy going into the White Mountains of California in the Eastern Sierra to commune with the bristlecone pine trees, some of which are more than 5,000 years old. Many of the bristlecones were young trees when Socrates was an old man. These trees of the White Mountains are the oldest living things on Earth, as far as I know. They are good company. They have seen it all. Besides being around when Socrates asked "Who am I" they were present when Job cried out "Why did all this bad stuff happen to me?"

There are moments when I am anxious about time passing and other moments when I view this reality with some serenity. I have not known anyone who got out of this life alive, and I do not think I will be an exception. My own mortality weighs upon me, sometimes heavily and sometimes more lightly.

The revelations of the astronomers and geologists in the last two hundred years tend to have a cool and composed demeanor that doesn't totally account for the slight pain of my own existence and the extreme pain in the lives of many people. Eons of time projected in the fossil record and the discovery of the "first humans" a few million years earlier than anticipated suggest a time frame difficult to image. The concept of a "light-year" away in astronomy is beyond the imagination, so vast is the space involved, yet many stars are projected to be incalculable light-years away. It is so difficult to comprehend the vastness of the universe as well as the long time line of the past. Where it all began is a further mystery. Perhaps the concept of beginning is in itself totally inadequate.

One wonder of my era is the Hubbell Telescope snapping photos of supernovas exploding, countless light-years away. Who could fail to find existence wondrously incomprehensible after becoming aware of the pictures from the Hubbell Telescope? One ingenious Christmas card of my time is a mapped satellite picture of light on earth, a panoramic photo that is passed around among my Internet friends during the Holiday Season. This is truly a portrait of the light of the world, with the major population centers as the main illuminators.

Sometimes I look at old photos of my children playing, at perhaps five years old, and wish fervently that somehow the moment could be alive forever, frozen in time, never moving forward. I have longed at times for such past moments, perhaps a day fishing or hunting with my beloved father. But I know that those moments will never return. Those moments are a memory, a precious but mere memory. Time proceeds inexorably forward. Time is not neutral.

There were moments in my 20s when I was anxious about where I might be at 35 in my career and my personal life. Then, as I passed 60, I looked back, and I saw where things had gone, and wondered if I would be around at 70 or 80. The time ahead is more finite than the time past, yet it is difficult to quantify. The past seems right there, the future seems right ahead. I know the future will be shorter than the past, so there is an awareness of the finite amount of time, but beyond that I know little about time.

In my travel publishing, I often return to places, perhaps years after my initial visit. I might cruise Alaska and then return a decade later. This is another aspect of time passing for me. When I return, I wonder if this will be my final visit. In my work, when selling travel photographs, I am constantly looking at my earlier photos, from perhaps 10–20 years ago, filled with my helpful travel friends, some of whom have died. These past images constantly impinge upon me.

It has taken me decades to comprehend the famous line by T. S. Eliot, "April is the cruelest month." Such a line could not have been written by or understood by a young person. As my mature years proceed, the poignancy has become greater with each returning spring, each new spring flowering of the plum tree in my condo yard.

Time is one of the great mysteries of life. I do not anticipate solving the mystery. Rather, I will ponder it and accept it, realizing that this mystery is a major part of what it means to be alive.

Cliff Palace ruins at Mesa Verde

CHAPTER FIFTEEN

Mesa Verde: The Anasazi's Meaning of Life

◡

*I*was exploring the world of the Anasazi, the "ancient ones," the name given to the cliff-dweller Native Americans at Mesa Verde National Park in Colorado. I spent a day climbing in and out of their homes, constructed of stone in the cliffs. They grew a surplus of beans, corn, and cotton in the fertile soil and reached relatively high population levels. Sometime around the 12th century, their culture declined, probably stressed by drought, which was a periodic check on all life-forms throughout the U.S. West.

In a museum at Mesa Verde, I saw some remarkable artifacts, preserved over the eons because of the dry environment. There were samples of the Anasazi foodstuffs, actual beans and corn from more than a thousand years ago. I saw cotton garments and decorous dog-hair belts they had woven. As a leisure culture, they had devoted a certain amount of time to their arts and crafts.

I wondered what life meant to a typical Anasazi person. I often speculate about what life means to different people. There is an element of imagination in what each person brings to life, plus, of course, the imaginative range of the culture into which they are born. Then there are the circumstances of life that shape a person directly.

My own perception of the meaning of life is therefore both alike and different from all other people, of my time and any previous time. I wonder what the Anasazi thought of life as they sat weaving their dog-hair belts. Moreover, there were other cultures that did not think it too important to create artifacts, such as the Miwok Indians of California.

So many basic things for an Anasazi were totally different from my life. They were dependent on natural light, while I can have light at any hour of the day or night. The images and experiences of their daily lives were almost totally of nature, while my world is filled with technology, machines, cities, and man-made artifacts. Their world was totally local, perhaps with a radius of 10 miles, while I have seen probably 100 countries around the globe. Perhaps they had few thoughts beyond a full belly, a good crop, and a healthy family.

I often feel that I have only a limited ability to approximate the mind-set of people in my own time and culture. How presumptuous that I could even begin to comprehend the Anasazi.

I have witnessed some imaginative ranges that other cultures brought to the meaning of life in my time.

I've met inland Eskimos at Anaktuvuk Pass in far northern Alaska, some of whom live on a diet of raw caribou and raw whale meat, eating no vegetables at all and only occasional berries in the spring and summer. Some of the older Eskimos I met recalled the long winters before the modern era, when there was very little light for several months.

The Acadians I've talked to in New Brunswick have somehow survived as an aggrieved people over two centuries as the English sought to deport them and suppress their Catholic religion.

Salsa dancers I've watched in Rio seemed to move with an innate suppleness and sensuality in their performance. Their world consisted totally of music and dance, nothing else mattered.

Young people I've encountered in Saint Petersburg knew of the treasures of the czars and their Summer Palace, but they have to live with an awareness that Soviet society can barely arrange basic food for its people.

I've observed Thai monks at Sukhothai go about their prayerful meditations, apparently totally secure in the assumption that someone will fill their rice bowls every day.

To many people living on the earth in my era, life is truly nasty, brutish, and short. I have seen the teeming slums of Rio and Cairo, where there is little hope for the basics of sufficient food, clean water, pure air, shelter, rudimentary education, and health care.

The people of history equally pique my curiosity as I seek to estimate what they must have felt about life.

I wonder what the Dead Sea Scroll people were thinking about life the day they wrapped up a manuscript in linen cloth and then sealed the contents in an earthen jar.

Pockets of culture have arisen in remote places. What were the Maori of New Zealand thinking when they concluded that displaying their tongues would be an effective mode of intimidation?

If I were continually looking at the snowy dome of an imposing mountain, like the Native Americans who lived near Mount Shasta in California, I too would probably conclude that the gods lived within it and that my own ancestors came from it.

The meaning of life would require a total assessment of the thoughts of all the people who had ever lived, now and yesterday. I could only begin to approximate the full truth of this wondrous matter.

Mount Denali (aka McKinley) in Alaska

CHAPTER SIXTEEN

Denali: The Beauty of Nature

I lurched along in an old school bus down the lonely road that is the only route into the great Alaska park, Denali. The bus ride took me a half day just to begin to get into the park. No personal cars are allowed in this mammoth park. I longed to get a view of "the great one" or Denali, also known as Mount McKinley.

On this trip the great white head of the mountain rose majestically against a bright blue sky. More often than not, I knew, the summit is shrouded in clouds from a ground-level perspective. When that was the case in past visits, I sometimes flew in a small plane on a bumpy aerial path around the mountain, buffeted by the chill downdraft winds that glaciers can cause. I watched as my bush plane pilot attentively eyed the mountain, which is big enough to cause its own weather.

I am at times anxious when faced with the more awesome aspects of nature. I gazed out at Mount McKinley in Alaska, and it gazed back, marvelous in all its aspects, but not caring much about me. Seeing Denali is one of the stupendous natural sights available on the planet. Similarly, I have watched the great herds migrate across the grasslands of Kenya, each animal concerned about its own survival, not too aware of me.

The beauty of nature is something that always energizes me. It might be a hillside of diverse wildflowers at Point Reyes in Northern California in the spring. It might be the recurring phenomena of the California Gray Whale migration, visible all along the California coast in January as the whales swim their annual epic journey. The whale trip is the longest mammal migration on earth, from the Arctic to Mexico. The whales feast during summer in chilly arctic waters and journey each winter to warm Scammons Lagoon in mid Baja to give birth to their calves and to mate.

Nature does not care about me, I realize. Nature is both beautiful and severe. Everything lives only for a time. Everything becomes part of the food chain. There is some playfulness in nature, especially when animals are in their prime, but the main activity is a struggle to survive. Plants compete for light, waging silent struggles in the forest to out-shade their competitors. This is all wondrous to behold, but it proceeds without any concern for my presence.

There is so much to learn about and delight in regarding nature. I regret that my time is so short. I will only have a few encounters with nature, but I will have more than most people. I always wish for more.

Sometimes I discovered natural beauty close to home. One autumn, for example, my travel editorial tasks took me by chance to see fall color in the California Sierra. I had not been in the mountains much in October in the past. I had assumed that California did not have a fall color that could rival Minnesota or New Hampshire. But I was mistaken. Driving Highways 88-89 south of Lake Tahoe, then cutting south on 395, and returning over the Sonora Pass, I saw a lavish display of reds and yellows in the aspen and cottonwood that was truly breathtaking. I hope to make such an autumn pilgrimage many times in the future.

Occasionally there have been ravishing natural sights that come alive in my feelings when I visit them again. One editorial project took me to the Big Sur coast of California, where I had been before. I walked again on Garrapata Beach and immersed myself in the pounding waves and tawny sand. Big Sur's gift of beauty to me was once again alive.

I am fortunate enough in my travel writing pursuits to see a spectrum of the natural beauty of the world.

Once, for several hours I flew by jet northward in Brazil from the grasslands of the Pantanal to Manaus in the heart of the Amazon. The jet traveled at about 500 miles per hour. I would look down, and there was the Amazon rain forest. I would look down again in an hour and the forest continued to extend in an unbroken manner to the horizon. Such was the vastness of the place. In Manaus I traveled by boat for a couple of days on the Amazon River, which was 10 miles wide at that location. It would be 200 miles wide at the mouth of the river, farther east. What an immense flow of water this represented.

The fecundity of animals on the plains of Kenya and in the great temperate forest at Yellowstone awed me. Because of the biomass of edible grass, the wildebeests in Kenya and the elk in Yellowstone can reach huge population levels. In Kenya I watched the closely entangled world of prey and predators, as lions lay in wait for passing herds of ungulates. In Jackson Hole, Wyoming, in January, I rode out in a horse-drawn sleigh to be amid the 5,000 elk that gather on the plains south of Yellowstone to endure the winter.

If I had to choose a single place in my experience to return to again and again for renewal of the sense of beauty in nature, it would be to Yosemite National Park in California, which I have visited in all four seasons over the years. The granite face of Half Dome provokes a hushed sense of natural majesty, as close as I have ever come to a cathedral in nature.

Kennedy Space Center in Florida

CHAPTER SEVENTEEN

Cape Canaveral: The Adventure of Space Flight

∿

I stood at Cape Canaveral in Florida in front of the towering rockets that have sent my species into space, for the first time ever, and it happened in my lifetime. The urge to do this, of course, had many origins. One year when I was in high school, the national debate subject was, "Resolved, that we should adopt the Russian system of education." The Sputnik launch of the Russians had shocked America to think that a rival could out-perform American scientific know-how. I won the Minnesota high school debate championship that year. I studied

Russian in college, partly because my father envisioned that there would be trade and friendship eventually between the United States and the then dreaded Soviet Communists.

Many years later, long after the Soviet competition had ended, I stood before the rockets at Canaveral. Like any traveler, I could see the rockets up close and personal. Canaveral is both a working launch site and a museum to this technology.

Like millions of others, I have visited the Smithsonian National Air and Space Museum in Washington, D.C., and have put my hand on an actual piece of rock from the moon. It is no accident that this branch of the Smithsonian is the most visited museum in the world. Space flight represents man's desire to know and do great things in our time. Getting to the moon has been a political competition also, but it is a win-win political struggle for all the citizens on Earth. Space flights produce many technical breakthroughs that are a tangible derivative of this competition. It is surely a marvel of human accomplishment that only 66 years passed between the first Wright Brothers flights at Kitty Hawk and the first human steps on the moon.

The journey into space is also a wondrous story of human cooperation on Earth, requiring an unprecedented social cohesion for the venture. Like the building of the great pyramids in Egypt, launching rockets is the work of many hands joined together. It is said that 250,000 Americans worked on various aspects of the project to send a man to the moon. In Egypt, I learned that the builders of the pyramids at Giza considered it a privilege and an honor to work on the project. Even if I have been only a small part of the 20th-century team, as a U.S. taxpayer funding the projects, I feel a pride and pleasure in the space flights. My cousin Jimmie has been one of the PhD mathematicians who make these things happen directly. Jimmie's career was at NASA in Mountain View, California, doing the rarified celestial calculations for satellite flights.

The view of Earth from space is unlike any other earlier view of Earth. This blue-green planet is so finite and forlorn, as seen from space. It is like a jewel or a treasure much in need of exquisite care. A limited carrying capacity for the Earth seems suddenly apparent, as in the metaphor of Spaceship Earth.

Launches spur education and wonder. They enlarge the imagination by stretching the concept of time and distance. The later manned orbital vehicles were populated by Americans, Russians, both men and women, and eventually by an ever widening spectrum of citizens from many countries, India to Israel.

Every day I benefit from the space satellites that assist in my communications with family, friends, and my editorial associates around the world. Every day I have worldwide news, information, and entertainment because of satellite technology.

The space program has also accomplished something never before imagined. It has sent an emissary from Earth to a milieu beyond our solar system. That was the *Pioneer 10* craft, with the bronze plaque showing a friendly man and woman, plus some mathematical notation that an alien might interpret. After 31 years of signal-sending, *Pioneer 10* finally beamed back its last, faint message to us, while hurtling ever onward in space.

The journey beyond Earth will always have its dangers, which a generation of schoolchildren learned when their teacher-astronaut died in the *Challenger* disaster. I have paused to salute this contribution at the *Challenger* headstone in the Arlington National Cemetery near Washington. In 2003 I participated in the national grief that followed the *Columbia* loss, when the shuttle broke up over Texas on reentry, killing another seven of the best and brightest of my species.

Space is a new imaginative frontier that the human animal needs. There was a time when European navigators strove to be the first to circle the globe. Captain James Cook actually received the title of The Great Circumnavigator. In the early years of the United States, Lewis and Clark led an expedition to discover the great lands of the West. Voyages of discovery, such as these, continue to fuel the imagination. Space has a similar appeal, both for its endless stretching of thought and its enormous potential practical benefits. Exploration beyond the Earth is destined to provide an endless and unconquerable frontier.

Canaveral suggests to me that if mankind is capable of such marvelous things as space flight, perhaps mankind can also accomplish seemingly simpler matters on Earth, such as creating more peace and prosperity.

A frigate bird in the Galápagos

CHAPTER EIGHTEEN

Galápagos: The Passions of the Biologists

❧

*T*he brevity and individuality of my own life, compared to the long continuum of life and the remarkable diversity of life-forms, was a mystery particularly poignant as I sailed in a small yacht through the Galápagos. I was reliving the voyages of Charles Darwin, moving from island to island, observing the slight variation in the birds, especially the finches, which evolved in isolation on the different islands. I thought about Darwin's time, and, somewhat earlier, the discoveries at the start of the 19th century of fossil bones from species that no longer existed. The notion that species were not permanent was a shock in itself at the time. The idea that species could change and evolve was a double mystery because no one could see this in their own lifetime.

There were places where the diversity of life-forms was a major experience. At the Monterey Bay Aquarium in California, for example, the wondrousness of jellyfish, such as the comb jellyfish, was on display. When I saw this exhibit, I felt overjoyed to be part of the cornucopia on Earth that included these creatures. In the rain forests of Costa Rica, my son Paul and I marveled at the complexity of plant and animal life all around us, rejoicing at being part of the pageant.

In my time there are many challenges with species getting inadvertently carried around the planet and filling niches. A righteous Sierra Club hiker can be traipsing through the Amazon one week, get a seed stuck in the mud of his boots, then introduce that seed accidentally the next week into the California environment, where it might be specially suited to take over aggressively. San Francisco Bay is now choked with an invasive small clam from Asia that is thought to have arrived in the pumped-out bilgewater of ships. Man's inadvertent acts of introducing invasive plants and animals rival man's bungled deliberate attempts. I think of tropical islands where the mongoose was introduced to catch rats, but instead it decimated the native bird population.

Biology is likely to be the dominant science of the 21st century, just as physics was the premier model of learning in the last century. I experienced biological breakthroughs at the time of the birth of my children. An amniocentesis test was made to confirm that there was no mental retardation in the fetus. A by-product of the test is information on the sex of the child. A modern parent knows if the child is a boy or a girl before birth, something never before known.

Only in my time, with advances in genetics, is man actually creating new life-forms, greatly accelerating the slow process of natural selection. In my time men have in fact become gods, with the ability to create species previously unheard of and unimagined. It is a heady responsibility for man to manage this task. However, once the knowledge exists, man just has to do it, hopefully for long-range benefit, irregardless of the risks. That is the nature of man.

I enjoyed visiting the house in Santa Rosa, California, of Luther Burbank. The "plant wizard," as he was called, did so much the old-fashioned way to develop new varieties of fruiting plants and grains, adding much to the base of California's agricultural wealth. But Burbank's techniques as a breeder of plants in the 19th century were conservative compared to the genetic-based creations of the 21st century.

With the new biology there is so much hope for solving real problems, which always outweighs the fear of errors. Above all, there is the hope of expanding the food supply, a desperate need for the millions on the brink of starvation. There is also the goal of new therapies for diseases. The progressive side of my sensibility allies itself with these hopes. Skilled management of the new genetic biology could unleash benefits that would mitigate real problems. Vitamin or protein elements might be introduced into basic grains, improving the nutrition.

However, I learned some cautionary things in my years as a food gardener, raising most of the vegetables for my family of five on a small lot in Oakland, California, culminating in my book *Backyard Farming*. I learned that man always underestimates the complexity needed for stability in the natural environment. The elegant simplicity of physics is totally unlike the messy complexity of biological

diversity. Man is never quite able to see the unintened consequences of manipulation of the environment. DDT was
introduced as a wonder pesticide, but gradually worked
its way up the food chain and nearly destroyed the rap-
tors, such as the peregrine falcon. Fortunately, the danger
was finally seen and corrected. Similarly, I wonder how
wise it is to breed bacillus thuringensis into plants so as
to reduce the loss of food crops to caterpillars. Would this
new plant also end up destroying the caterpillars of the
monarch butterfly, as an example?

I am part of the onrushing, evolving life force. Perhaps,
soon, life-forms on other planets or in other galaxies will
be confirmed. Whether man on Earth has the wisdom to
manage the godlike powers to create new species is a question that only future observers can answer in retrospect.

Pyramids at Giza, Egypt

CHAPTER NINETEEN

Egypt: The Accomplishments of Man

∽

When visiting Egypt I was fortunate to be among the 120 people a day who are allowed into the special tomb of Nefertari. The issue is acidic moisture from human breath corrupting the artworks. The vivid colors in the tomb of Nefertari, from the 12th century B.C., but only recently discovered, are simply stunning. It seems as if the painters have stepped out for a momentary cup of coffee and will soon be back. The paint is that fresh, the colors that exquisite. Throughout Egypt there are many

other colossal creations, even beyond the well-known pyramids at Giza. There are the huge statues of Ramses II
on the upper Nile, carved in stone, meant solely to intim-
idate any invaders who might be sailing down the Nile
from Sudan. In the Cairo Museum I saw the treasures
from the tomb of Tutankhamen, with their delicate ranges of craftsmanship, everything that a regal person would
need in the afterlife.

Some of the greatest accomplishments of mankind in-
volve how people populated various parts of the globe. In
Hawaii I learned about the *Hokulea,* a deep-sea voyaging
canoe built in 1975 to re-create the trips from the Marque-
sas and Tahiti to Hawaii, which started in roughly A.D.
250. In these voyages ancient people discovered Hawaii,
one of the most remote places on earth, approximately
2,500 miles from the nearest inhabited place. How people
ever got to Hawaii is a marvel to contemplate.

The people of the South Pacific had no knowledge
of where land would be. They only knew that certain
birds, such as the golden plover, flew from the north and
returned to the north. These birds could not land in water,
so there must be terra firma up there, somewhere, where
they could end their flight. One wonders how many such

canoes, sailing north, missed Hawaii and perished in the abyss of the oceans and time, lost forever, or sailed all the way north to Alaska. In fact, modern DNA studies suggest that the Haida people in Alaska are part of a genetic heritage that came from the South Pacific, past Hawaii. So it is likely that some voyaging canoes missed the islands entirely and sailed on to Alaska.

Mankind's current accomplishments in the 20th-21st centuries take so many forms. I enjoy traveling in the spring through the Central Valley of California, when the fruit trees are in blossom. The Central Valley is a breadbasket of the world, the amazingly fecund heart of the most productive agricultural state in the country. California is sometimes said to be the sixth biggest economy in the world, depending on how one measures things. Agriculture is a hefty part of the story. In the Central Valley I see some of the most skillful farming currently practiced on Earth. Ranching and farming families, including my own cousins, make this possible. As I write this, my cousin, Will Jr., is Secretary of Agriculture for California.

The critical artifacts and art objects showing accomplishments of the great past civilizations delight me whenever I have a chance to make their acquaintance.

In Mexico City I immersed myself in the National Museum of Anthropology, which displays treasures from the Aztec, Maya, and other earlier peoples of Mexico. I did this at a time when the Hispanic population of California surpassed Blacks as the most numerous minority. In 50 years there will be more Hispanics than Whites in California. If everyone were required to visit the National Museum of Anthropology, there would be no prejudice against Mexicans, who, I feel, are capable of artistic greatness equal to any world culture. The elaborate gold creations of early Peru are a similar treasure.

In Oslo I marveled at the 9th-century Viking ships. The Vikings were the most impressive European sailors of their era. They acquired silk from China, though they didn't know enough about basic hygiene to prevent their endemic stomach problems.

The architecture of Thailand's three historic capitals (Sukhothai, Ayuthaya, and Bangkok) equals the grandeur of anything I have seen. The significant artistic creative moments, especially in sculpture, such as the graceful depiction of the Buddha in the Sukhothai period, parallel all stellar artistic accomplishment in Europe or the Americas.

The destruction of human accomplishments fills me with malaise. How I wish that the grand Library of Alexandria had not been burned in ancient times. I wish I could have prevented the Spanish Catholic clergymen in Mexico from torching the great Mayan literature, such as the *Popul Vuh.* How sad I felt on the Norway coast to learn that the retreating Germans had methodically dynamited every building of every coastal town as they withdrew during World War II. That the Taliban in Afghanistan felt compelled to blow up huge ancient Buddhas is one of the recent tales in this sad catalog of cultural destruction.

Accomplishments of many types are an ongoing contribution in the continuum of human life. Prometheus got mythic credit for capturing fire. Someone at an early date invented the wheel. Human accomplishments in all forms are a wondrous matter to celebrate.

Little things I appreciate

CHAPTER TWENTY

Berkeley: The Little Things I Appreciate

~

When backpacking in the Yosemite High Country of California, I am reminded of the little things I appreciate every day as a modern man at my condo in Berkeley. After a few days of backpacking, I like returning home from this more primitive man-against-the-elements setting.

In Berkeley I can take a hot shower every day, something no king could have done in earlier times.

I can banish the dark with electric lights, something no one would have dreamed of 150 years ago.

I can heat my space easily on a cold day with a gas furnace, something that would have been much more difficult a few centuries ago.

I can wash and dry clothes with a machine, effortlessly.

I can go to the local Safeway food market, or the more specialized Verbrugge meat/fish and Yasai produce shops, and select a range of fresh, nutritious, and varied food that is without precedent in human history. Much of this food is "sourced" at exotic worldwide locations and transported at huge cost, but this is a marvel of my time.

I can put a chilled ice cube in a glass of water on a hot day, something impossible 150 years ago.

Millions of people live in air-conditioned comfort in distressed high-heat areas. In Berkeley, I do not need air-con. But when I go to Arizona or Florida on a summer travel research trip, I do enjoy this amenity, which makes civilized life possible in these comfort-distressed climates.

I have clean water to drink from the Mokelumne River watershed, arguably some of the purest water in the world.

I can communicate easily with my sisters in Indonesia or Minnesota by phone or by email over the Internet. With my laptop in tow and my home phone forwarded to my cell phone, my "office" can be anywhere in the world.

I have access to news, opinions, and entertainment from throughout the global village via my TV, radio, Internet connection, and CD player. I can log in on my computer to read the *New York Times* at will.

I have the possibility of remarkable medical intervention that can extend my life. For instance, I experienced a skin cancer on my skull that would probably have proven debilitating and eventually fatal only a generation ago. Modern skin-cancer surgery solved my problem.

I can heat beverages or food in a microwave oven, in minutes, so much faster than fossil-fuel heating methods of earlier times.

I can travel around the planet by airplane, a magical matter that never ceases to amaze me. On the local scene, I can transport myself in a self-propelled vehicle, the automobile.

Though the world around me is hardly at peace, I enjoy a special tranquil environment. I live in a happy little condo-association in Berkeley. I own the upper half of a house. The floor below me belongs to Lynne, a talented designer. On the property there is a cottage in the back.

This happens to be owned by John, whose existence and livelihood is surely a statement about the times. John is a world-class chess champion and author of some 13 books on chess. John has one of the two paid positions in the United States to do nothing but play chess and organize chess tournaments. This is at the Mechanics Institute, a post–Gold Rush library set up in San Francisco by someone who struck it rich and liked chess. Condo associations can be a living hell, but my condo scene in Berkeley consists of congenial partners.

Of course, there are many challenges and stresses, some small and some large, for the modern people of my time.

I have to deal with modern technology, such as the computer, which is terrific when it works and frustrating when it breaks down. I have to master ongoing "learning curves."

I have to deflect or delete the hundred or so "spam" messages I receive each day in email. Sometimes I do this deletion during the dinner hour and have to pick up the persistently ringing phone to tell some cold-call intruder that I do not want the offered mortgage-refinancing pitch. Only after enough people became sufficiently irritated were the telemarketers restrained by the law.

Though I work at home, others have to develop the resilience to withstand long car or public transportation commutes to get to work. Anyone flying on an airplane after 9-11-01 needs to submit to time-consuming security searches.

One thing I enjoy every day is some chilled Chardonnay wine. I think of the trenches I saw in the chalk soil of Bordeaux at Château Ausone. Ausonius had been a Roman poet and had ordered those trenches dug and vines planted in the 4th century. Wine does not cause me to speak in tongues. That would be too ambitious. However, wine does elevate my awareness and causes me to rejoice in the wonder and beauty of life, even as the realities of life sometimes impinge on this loftier vision. A glass of wine is one of the many little things I appreciate.

Flowers in Hawaii

CHAPTER TWENTY-ONE

Honolulu: The Sensuality of Life

◠

Each day in my daily life, but especially when I travel to Hawaii, I am reminded of the pleasure of life's sensuality. When I disembark the airplane, a lei is put around my neck. Leis are sometimes made of vanda orchids or of plumeria. The perfume of the lei and the warm tropical air of Hawaii immediately bathe me. A range of bright flowers can be seen everywhere, starting with bougainvillea or hibiscus, the state flower, giving a Technicolor aura to Hawaii. Brightly floral aloha shirts, which appear ostentatious on the mainland, seem immediately appropriate here.

I look around the airport in Honolulu and observe the people. The most striking aspect of the people is that their racial origins are diverse and are primarily from the South Pacific and Asia. Aside from the Portuguese, the main groups are Polynesian, Japanese, Chinese, and Korean. This mixture of races has produced women of legendary beauty, with coal black eyes and olive thighs, who hula dance through the longings of the male visitor. Of course, the men are handsome also, as the woman visitor may conclude when observing the rippling muscles of the beachboy paddling the outrigger canoe. Men were originally the only sex allowed to dance the hula.

Adding to the sensuality of people I experience in Hawaii is the tropical greenery that grows so luxuriously in the warm, bright sun and moist air. Imagine the thoughts of a visitor from Minnesota, in winter, who has been thinking of the windchill factor only a day earlier, suddenly alighting in Hawaii, where the temperature at sea level varies only from 63 to 85 degrees all year round. For many visitors, the predictable warmth and benign sun are sufficient to breathe life into the word paradise. While Alaskans suffer a dark night of the soul through the winter, Hawaiians luxuriate in sunlight and warmth.

Hawaiians distinguish winter from summer by discerning that the weather is a few degrees cooler and the rains are slightly more frequent.

With a snorkel mask I realize how this tropically rich sensuality extends to the world below sea level. Coral, multicolored fish, and giant green sea turtles present an otherworldly sight. Only Florida, within the United States, can compete with Hawaii as a tropical landscape above and below sea level. In Hawaii there is intense color in the land, sea, and sky. Besides the coral and the fish, I find pleasure in some lava-red sunsets in this land of eternal June. All visitors and natives can enjoy these sunsets from the beaches in an egalitarian celebration of nature. All of the beaches of Hawaii are owned by all of the people, all of the time.

I do not have to travel, however, to enjoy the sensuality of life. It is around me every day in great abundance, and I savor it.

I enjoy what I drink every day, starting with the rich French Roast coffee of each morning. At lunch or dinner there is chilled Chardonnay. In the late evening I favor green tea.

I appreciate what I eat every day, such as the texture and taste of baked salmon. Small leaves of arugula lend a smoky taste to a spinach salad. Some taste pleasures are so simple, like the clean, repeatable taste of fresh rice. I seldom go through a day without ingesting some garlic, ginger, and pepper.

I love to listen to music, and I usually listen to "love songs after dark" in the evening on my local station, KOIT Lite Rock, Less Talk radio. I listen to music at the Y while I walk for a brisk 20 minutes on the cardio treadmill, set at a 3.5 percent grade, 3.8 miles per hour. Exercising my body in this moderate way is a major pleasure, especially when followed by a hot shower.

The climate in Berkeley is usually fresh and cool. The sun is ample and bright, but not overly hot, for most of the year. There are few mosquitoes or other biting insects in the relatively arid Bay Area. During the winter rains, I enjoy the cozy warmth of my condo as the winds howl and the rains fall. There is much pleasure in my environment, which has little of the extreme cold or searing heat of other locales.

The presence of a woman in my life, when that occurs, accentuates all the pleasures of life. To me a woman can be the epitome and ultimate expression of all things sensual.

The measured pace of my day also has a special sensuality. I have to focus on my literary and photographic projects, but the pace is never frantic. There is always time for pleasurable aspects every day. I work intently, knowing that there will be that cardio workout with music in the evening at the Y. There is something hypnotic about the anticipation.

I feel it is fortunate that I am not an angel, which, by definition, would have made me devoid of bodily sensuality.

Dubrovnik in the former country Yugoslavia

CHAPTER TWENTY-TWO

Yugoslavia: The Legacy of Religions

〜

I traveled through Yugoslavia just before everything became unraveled. I remember sitting with my fellow journalists at press conferences, trying to figure out what was going on. Within a year the Christians and the Muslims would be killing each other, except when the Christians were killing other Christians.

In Belgrade, I learned how the city had been overrun something like 25 times in the last 20 centuries as the Muslim or "heathen" forces from the east fought with the Christian or "Crusader" forces from the west, sailing up and down the Danube. It would soon happen again. In another year the Christian Serbs would slaughter 7,500 Muslim men and boys in the village of Srebrenica alone. Combatants would do their best to destroy with artillery the jewel of a seaside city, Dubrovnik, heedless of the great artistic heritage they were decimating.

I feel a major ambivalence toward the main religions of the world, though there are also ironies. Religions are among the institutions that teach literacy and can preserve culture, things I value highly. The Koran and the Bible contribute to the literacy motivations of many people. They can be the first writings to learn. I will always have a deep appreciation for the Arab religious scholars who preserved the writings of the Greeks while Europe suffered its Dark Ages. Without those Arab clerical scholars, the questions of Socrates, the thoughts of Aristotle, and the poetry of Homer would have been lost forever.

What disturbs me is the cultural superiority that religion instills in the faithful. In my own California the Spanish Catholics wiped out the Native American culture because of the assumed superiority of Christianity. The Maya culture of Mexico, with its rich poetic artifacts, was similarly eradicated to the best of the ability of the conquerors. Certain elements of Christianity today tend to demonize the Muslims after 9-11.

Tensions within my spirit arise over the conflict that there are too many people, with resulting harmful effects on the environment, and religion is partly responsible for this situation. One of my silent arguments with the Catholic Church has been over the Church policy preventing the dissemination of birth control information. I saw the effect of this in Catholic Mexico. I saw oil-rich Mexico in the energy-expensive 1970s make some progress in its effort to provide food, health care, and education for its masses, but every gain was offset by the exploding population. The Catholic Church had such a grip on the culture that birth control remained a taboo.

The three major political worries of my time are fueled by religious fanaticism. They are the Jew versus Muslim Arab struggle in the Middle East, the general rising tide of Muslim versus "Crusader" Christian America and Europe throughout the world, and the Hindu versus Muslim conflict along the India-Pakistan border. Any of these three struggles can result in conflagrations that will upset the civilized patterns of the world. A minor player, armed with the compact tools of mass destruction, the advance chemical-biological-radiological arsenals of my time, can destroy numerous humans.

Fanaticism, something that I or any other human being is capable of, is the culprit. I feel that fanaticism lies dormant in every human being, threatening to awaken. I remember the sweat that broke out over my body as a boy when the Catholic nuns and priests in Minnesota described the vividness of Hell. Burning in Hell for All Eternity was the ultimate bad thing. Therefore, anything Evil in the world that might encourage this Damnation, especially any threat to the Faith, was anathema. From a theological point of view, even the Lutherans of Minnesota were seen as deficient when it came to understanding the Catholic truth. Beyond Minnesota, of course, there was Atheist Communist Russia, which might prevail. The faithful prayed a rosary weekly for the conversion of Russia.

I could see later how easily this fanaticism might have developed if my own relatively enlightened and comfortable Minnesota world had been different. If I had lived a life of poverty and political despair, the norm throughout much of the world in my time, surely some force in the world must be responsible for my wretched fate, and might that not be the most powerful and wealthy nation in the world, the United States? I understood that I might have been capable of a jihad against this tactile target. I saw how men of vision could propel the fanatical person forward, just as Pope Urban II unleashed generations of Crusaders to rescue the Holy Land.

In my time, those growing up without political or theological passion seem to need a video-game or sports fantasy world of fanaticism to possibly exorcise, even while dangerously feeding, this impulse. In Oakland-Berkeley, the Black Hole of the Raiders NFL football team provides fantasy bonding for some in a Superbowl context. It is unlike the ballpark at Mexico's Chichén Itzá, where the losing team lost not only the game, but also life itself. I look at the Raiders Black Hole fans on television with some mild disgust at their make-believe, low-life antics, but I know that I could be capable of fanatic excesses in real life too.

I. M. Pei Bank of China Building, Hong Kong

CHAPTER TWENTY-THREE

Hong Kong: The Accumulation of Wealth

❧

I often marvel at the hard work that human beings perform around the globe to survive and provide for their families. Hong Kong is the epitome of this urge to accumulate wealth. Every available surface in the city is in use for advertising. Throughout my travels I noticed that the Chinese enclaves, such as Cholon in Saigon, are centers of thrift and prosperity in the foreign cultures where the Chinese settled.

Sometimes I met people working in situations where there was little hope of progress. Outside of Manaus on the Amazon River in Brazil, I visited subsistence fishermen who caught a few small fish and raised a starchy root, called manioc, to trade in the market in Manaus for a meager income. These people fished most of the time.

In my era and world, work takes on some new aspects. Some work still requires primarily the ability to do a physical task, such as Federal Express people handling packages between me and editors. These workers need a good attitude to repeat their rounds day after day. I suspect that each of them can see some small gain with each package delivered.

Many jobs around me require ever higher skill levels. Most children need to go through college or more. Comfort levels with computers have to be great. The ability to write a clear sentence is important. The social skills to function in a group are primary. The patience to process information for long hours in front of a computer screen is elementary. The ability to endure a long commute is often a requirement.

Jobs in my time are not secure. Of course, as a freelance writer and photographer, I always accepted that. I always had to prove my worth, and I had assumed that mind-set. But many people who thought they had secure jobs were mistaken. I remember the day when some of my comrades employed at Sunset Publishing received their pink slips. Sunset, a Menlo Park, California, publisher with once womb-to-tomb security, was bought by Time Warner. Awhile later, things got shaken up. People who had worked at Sunset for 25 years and assumed they could coast, were let go.

There were times when jobs were plentiful, as in the dot-com prosperity in the late 1990s. Then there were times of shrinkage, when life was more difficult.

I flourish within a special group of workers, the content people, who create the writing and photography for American media, publishing in magazines, newspapers, books, and on the Internet. My group is engaged in a long struggle with publishers, from 1970 to the present, and the content people are gradually losing the struggle. The price paid for my work in the 1970s was higher than it is 30 years later.

The products that I and my colleagues create are special products, which can be replicated and reused. While I could sell an article or a photo for onetime rights to one magazine in 1970, the publisher in the 21st century says, "We'll pay you the same amount as for the use in one magazine, but as we own 20 magazines, let us use it in all of them, and on our website, and wherever else we might be able to sell it. We'll just own it. Take it or leave it, either as work for hire or sell us all rights."

I am fortunate to have created enough content that I own and therefore can resist the suicidal terms required by many modern publishers. But younger workers in my content field are destined never to own much, never to make much progress, and therefore never to fully exert themselves to do their best work. Consumers suffer because the quality of the content they view is diminished.

I and my fellow content providers look with some envy at our comparable colleagues, the doctors, lawyers, professors, and other professionals who have similar education and a similar level of expertise and attention. These other people are paid well if they show up for work and perform reasonably well. American society needs one person in each of these other professions for perhaps 100-500 people in the general population. But content workers are in a special situation. Their creations could be replicated, as if the work of one doctor could now service thousands or even millions of patients. I live out a situation unimaginable to other professions.

Surviving in the creative world of the content provider requires much focus. Some of my colleagues are living off their trust funds or their pensions, doing this creative work with less of a need to produce income. But my situation is different. I have wonderful children who merited college and graduate school support. I have family members who have lost their income-producing potential because of medical challenges. I have had less-than-smooth romantic entanglements that ended with marital partners going their separate ways, which always meant that the standard of living for everyone fell lower.

From some points of view, I live a genial existence of genteel poverty, traveling, photographing, and writing. But it requires a huge amount of marketing energy and ingenuity to survive. And, as I look ahead, the golden years will be golden only if I am able to maintain this pace of work.

Gruhn Guitar Shop in Nashville

CHAPTER TWENTY-FOUR

Nashville: The Urge to Create

O ne April I found myself in Nashville at the annual Tin Pan South celebration of singers and songwriters. A lot of American songs come out of the Nashville scene. I enjoyed a week of hearing music and listening to the stories of songwriters about how they created the music, even if someone else happened to popularize it.

One song that I like to listen to in the evening while walking on my treadmill at the Y is Bonnie Rait doing "I Can't Make You Love Me If You Don't." I listened in Nashville to that song sung by its actual creator, Mike Reid, who happened also to be an ex-NFL football star, play-ing five years with the Cincinnati Bengals. Reid described how he wrote the song. One morning Reid noticed in the newspaper an unusual story. It was a court report about some rustic area of Tennessee. Apparently, there was a lov-ers' dispute in that backwoods scene between a man and a woman, as is known to happen occasionally. The man did something foolish. He got out his shotgun and shot up the lady's car. No one was hurt, but property was damaged. He was arrested and found guilty. At his sentencing, the judge asked him if he had anything to say for himself. He said, "You just can't make a woman love you if she don't." Songwriter Reid let this bubble around in his imagination for a few months. Finally, out popped the song.

In the lyrics of song I find a lot of truths. Phrases of songs course through my mind. "There's a danger in lov-ing too much." "I will remember you, will you remember me?" "Thank you for the best day of my life." "What a wicked thing you do, to make me fall in love with you." Or I find myself dwelling on the reality of "Ain't no sun-shine when you're gone" or "I love you just the way you are" or "How can I live without you?" I sometimes find myself filled with such simple but pervasive thoughts as

"You fill my heart with gladness, you take away all my sadness, that's what you do."

I feel that the creation of anything is an audacious act. I do not define creativity in a narrow way. One can be creative in business, in law, in technology, in politics, in the making and nurturing of children, in shaping the direction of one's life, in human relationships generally. But the creation of artistic artifacts, such as songs, writings, photographs, movies, paintings, and sculptures are of a somewhat different order.

Such creative acts produce things that are not utilitarian and are not strictly necessary, though anyone who knows their value will argue they are more essential than bread on the table. Such acts, if not completed, will never be missed. The world will go on without them, not knowing of its impoverishment. These acts also put the creator at risk of failure if no audience ever appreciates them, though the truly committed artist will not let that be a deterrent to creation. Such acts are lonely acts, by definition, because no one compels the artist to create them. Some artifacts are also not appreciated in their own time, of which many examples could be cited, such as the paintings of van Gogh.

I have arranged my own life to be directly engaged in making such artistic artifacts, doing writing and photography directly about life, rather than pursuing a more reflective role in academia, where I would have ended up developing books about books. I like the rawness of life and direct experience, believing I learn more from direct experience than from once-removed observations about experience. I cherish my own opportunities to make artifacts, whether with writing or photography. If I make even a small number of minor artifacts that prove of value to my audience, then I feel my own life is worthwhile.

Whether the creative juices flow more from joy or from pain is an open question. I remember how the great 18th-century English writer, Samuel Johnson, wrote his seminal novel, *Rasselas,* in one week. Johnson wrote the novel quickly because he needed money to bury his mother. His publisher agreed to make the payment upon delivery of a novel-length manuscript. Johnson wrote furiously, as his mother lay patiently in her coffin.

My own creative efforts come more out of joy than out of pain. I have some joys in life, such as the existence of my children, my sisters, the woman in my life, the congenial Berkeley scene, my own good health, and the great garden of the world where I wander in my travels. But there is also tension in my world. Always there is the reality of surviving in the inadequately financed marketplace of the content providers. I have had many generous impulses toward those I love, but I lacked the means to express myself with material things. Beyond that there were the stresses specific to the decades, such as the Vietnam War of the 60s–70s, the energy shortage traumas of the 70s–early 80s, and then the environmental, political, and health (such as HIV) issues of the 80s–90s. I always felt tension, but it was energy-giving rather than some debilitating drain.

I would be comfortable with the epitaph, "He appreciated the urge to create."

Women at a Masai village in Kenya

CHAPTER TWENTY-FIVE

Kenya: The Prospect of a Long Life

One of the informative trips in my travel writing career has been a look at Kenya. The plentitude of large mammals in the grasslands was the dominant experience. However, the other memorable encounter I had was at a village of Masai in the Masai Mara area. I was able to go to their village and spend a day with them. They lived by tending their cows and goats on the plains. Their houses were made of sticks and animal dung. Their artifacts were few, mainly bright clothing, cooking utensils, and spears. They drank the blood from their cows and the milk from their cows and goats. They had a clever way of opening up the vein of a cow to drink the blood and then patching the hole with a wad of dung. Occasionally, they butchered an animal for meat. They spent a lot of time swatting at flies.

What most struck me about the villagers was the rapid parade of life unfolding around me, especially as I looked at the women. The girls were children until about the age of 12. Then they became women and started childbearing. They were in their prime until about age 20. By 25 they were already starting to look old. By 35 they were looking quite old. I wondered how long they lived.

As I look at myself, I wonder how long I will live. No one knows how many years he or she still has left. As of age 60 my statistical prospect is to live till age 82, based on the actuarial tables. I watched my grandfather live vigorously to age 94, dying at 96.

The phenomenon of many people living rather long lives is a new experience in my time. If one gets past childhood diseases, and most North Americans do in my time, then the prospect of a fairly long life is likely. This presents many opportunities and challenges. The older people need to learn how to pass their time in an enriching manner. The younger people need to produce more to provide the goods and services required by the older people. The younger people know that they too will ultimately become the older people. Actually, in my time, Italy has the most lopsided projection of older vs younger people among the developed nations. Ironically, even the Pope, so lacking in concern about the population explosion in the Third World, recognizes that there is a "low birthrate crisis" in Italy.

The likely length of life in California today is a major contrast with life expectancy here 200 years ago. I often think of the Ohlone Indians as they lived in an earlier California scene sometimes called a Golden Age. They had an abundance of food, easily gathered, consisting of acorns from the oak trees, shellfish, and fish. They pounded and ground the acorns with rocks to mash the hard kernels into a rough meal, which they then leached of tannins in water. They had one problem, however. Grains of rock flecked off with each pounding. Their teeth constantly ate the grains with each bite of the acorn meal. This sand wore down their teeth, causing illness and debilitation. They had a life expectancy of perhaps 30 years maximum, as opposed to my 80.

I realize that it is luxurious to live a long life, considering what has happened to so many young men in history, perishing especially in war. I remember the loneliness in my friend Mike's house in Minnesota after Mike's dad went off to the Korean War and never returned. I choked back my own emotions in Washington, D.C., when I visited the Vietnam War Memorial with my children. The grief managers there assisted me in making a rubbing of the name of my best high school friend, George, who had gone on to West Point and thence to Vietnam, not coming back under his own power. Especially in my travels through the U.S. South, at places like Franklin, Tennessee, and Vicksburg, Mississippi, the palpable sense of tragic death of the 600,000 men who died in the Civil War lay like a thick fog over the landscape.

I will probably live out a long life and probably die a natural death. Sometimes I view my eventual death with a certain tranquillity, aware of the processes in nature that I have observed so often. Most dramatic of all was my experience of watching salmon on their final migration upstream to spawn, lay eggs, and die, sometimes turning bright red in the process. I saw this many times, especially in Alaska, where there were thousands of salmon in the Chilkat River as I rafted along. I will be like the salmon, living energetically in my prime for a time, definitely spawning on a few joyous occasions, then resigning myself to my death and decay. But I will go on in some form, just as the salmon continue, both as new salmon in the next hatch and as part of the eagle or the grizzly bear that feeds on the dying salmon. I will be a joyous part of the eternal cycle of nature. Death will be something to accept rather than to struggle against.

ORDER FORM: Foster Travel Publishing

	QTY	PRICE
TRAVEL LITERATURE: Autographed		
Travels in an American Imagination:		
The Spiritual Geography of Our Time		
(Foster Travel Publishing)		
$14.95 ISBN 0-9760843-0-9 as book	_____	_____
and		
$14.95 on CD ISBN 0-9760843-1-7.	_____	_____
and		
$14.95 as online download ISBN 0-9760843-2-5	_____	_____
GUIDEBOOK: Autographed		
Northern California History Weekends		
(Globe Pequot)		
$15.95 ISBN 0-7627-1076-4	_____	_____
GUIDEBOOK: Autographed		
Adventure Guide to Northern California		
(Hunter Publishing)		
$15.95 ISBN 1-55650-821-2		
(Now between printings, new edition in 2006)	_____	_____
GUIDEBOOK: Autographed		
Making the Most of the Peninsula		
$12.95 ISBN 0-9760843-3-3	_____	_____
GUIDEBOOK: Autographed		
San Francisco and Northern California		
$12.95 ISBN 0-9760843-7-6	_____	_____
ENVIRONMENT: Autographed		
Backyard Farming		
$6.95 ISBN 0-9760843-4-1	_____	_____
FICTION: Autographed		
The Message of April Fools		
$9.95 ISBN 0-9760843-5-X.	_____	_____
MEMOIR: Autographed		
Just 25 Cents and Three Wheaties Boxtops		
$9.95 ISBN 0-9760843-6-8.	_____	_____
SUBTOTAL.		_____
8.75% California Sales Tax, if applicable.		_____
Shipping/handling:		
$3.50 first book, $2.00 additional book		_____
TOTAL		_____

Payment must be by check, credit card, or Paypal (to lee@fostertravel.com) at the time of order.

See other side for more information . . .

SEND ORDERS TO:

Foster Travel Publishing
P.O. Box 5715
Berkeley, CA 94705
Phone: (510) 549-2202 Fax: (510) 549-1131
Email: lee@fostertravel.com
Website: www.fostertravel.com

SEND BOOKS TO:

Name: _____

Address: _____

City, State, Zip: _____

Phone: _____ Email: _____
Details on how book(s) should be autographed:

_____

_____

CREDIT CARD PAYMENT — Lee Foster will process payment through ProPay:

❏ VISA or ❏ MasterCard #: _____

Expiration Date (month/year): _____/_____

Name as it appears on card: _____

Amount Authorized: _____

This form is online at www.fostertravel.com/orderform.pdf

About the Author

Lee Foster began his publishing career with a novel about the Vietnam era, *The Message of April Fools,* and a literary memoir about growing up in a Minnesota America at mid century, *Just 25 Cents and Three Wheaties Boxtops.* He was part of the energy-efficient-living/urban-organic-gardening movement in California, which he described in his book *Backyard Farming.* He has been known in recent decades for his award-winning travel writing/photography.

He was the first travel writer ever to publish profitably in the new electronic online scene, starting in 1983 with Compu-Serve, a contract that continued until 2001. His work has won seven Lowell Thomas Awards,including being named Lowell Thomas Travel Journalist of the Year (Silver Winner). His Foster Travel Publishing website (www.fostertravel. com) presents more than 200 destination articles with photos on his worldwide travels.

Lee Foster hiking Swiss Glaciers

As a travel photographer, he has images in more than 225 Lonely Planet books. His most recent Lowell Thomas Award was for his travel guidebook, *Northern California History Weekends* (Globe Pequot).

Contact Information:
Lee Foster, Foster Travel Publishing
P.O. Box 5715, Berkeley, CA 94705
(510) 549-2202
email: lee@fostertravel. com
www.fostertravel.com